'This is an engaging and vital read for any mo[...] to make their mark. This book is a practical, [...] for success embedded in real-world case stu[...] and shape our industry for the better. This book is for every ma[...] wants to step beyond boring work into truly brave and original thinking. If you're going to read one great book this year, make it this one.'
Pete Markey, Chief Marketing Officer, Boots

'I love this book! As B2B marketers, we've all had the experience of having our wings clipped, our creativity stifled. Choueke asks the hard questions, confronts traditional B2B principles, and pushes us to do better. This book should be required reading for all B2B marketers.'
Desiree Motamedi, Senior Global Marketing Director, Workplace at Facebook

'In *Boring2Brave* Mark takes a broadsword to the tyranny of mediocrity and perceived inferiority that pervades B2B marketing. An impassioned manifesto encouraging us to challenge our institutionalised timidity and take the power of bravery very seriously indeed.'
Adam Morgan, partner, eatbigfish and author of *Eating the Big Fish: How Challenger Brands Can Compete Against Brand Leaders*

'A joyous reminder that B2B marketing doesn't need to be the ugly sister of B2C. *Boring2Brave* is packed with thought-starters, real examples and anecdotes to empower marketing leaders and teams to deliver bigger and braver brand strategies… and it's the perfect guide for every CEO or founder trying to understand the role marketing can play in growth.'
Laura Pleasants, VP, Global Marketing, Captify

'With the help of some hard-earned wisdom, Choueke seeks to liberate B2B marketing from the shackles of caution, dull convention and uber-rationalism. *Boring2Brave* offers a manifesto for restlessness, creativity, storytelling and fun. Whether you're up-and-coming or an established B2B marketer, if you aspire to be better or dare to be different, read this book.'
Marc Nohr, Group CEO, Miroma Group Agencies, Honorary Fellow IPA and IDM

'A rowdy but charming hoodlum of a business book, *Boring2Brave* ripples with a seething anger, cloaked in easy-going humour and companionable storytelling. It's a style that makes for a monstrously effective weapon as Choueke takes swing after swing at the reprehensible mediocrity he sees across his beloved B2B marketing arena.'
Sam Conniff, author of *Be More Pirate*

'Mark writes with clarity, imagination and authority. Taking a category in which the default has been a lazy approach to brand and marketing, we now have a new operating system for B2B – brilliant!'
Amelia Torode, Co-Founder, The Fawnbrake Collective

'MarTech vendors all look and talk exactly the same; and in a language that's completely unrecognizable to that spoken by the brands they're trying to win as customers. This book captures something that's immediately apparent, yet completely unrealized: if a B2B company competed purely on the dimension of not coming off like every other boring-ass B2B, they'd immediately differentiate themselves in ways product, sales or service teams typically can't. *Boring2Brave* shows you the treasure map, it's up to you to take the journey.'

Reilly Dunn, Senior Enterprise Account Executive, Slack

'Few business books are this funny and engaging. Choueke knows how to tell the sort of stories you might share with friends on a night out while losing none of the inspiration and practical tips to make *Boring2Brave* a high-value read. A smart, vital and galvanising tool for B2B marketers everywhere.'

Anthony Eskinazi, Founder and CEO, JustPark

'A fast-paced and very readable call-to-arms full of wisdom, stories and quotable lines. Choueke puts into words a lot of things that many B2B marketers feel in their bones, and lays out clearly what ails the B2B marketing discipline, what can be done about it, and why it should be done. The case he builds, for creativity through bravery, is needed.'

**Jason Patterson, Content Strategy
Director and Co-Founder, IGNITE Global Marketing**

'A practical but passionate polemic that provides a roadmap for B2B marketers to realise untapped potential.'

**Russell Parsons, Editor-in-chief, *Marketing Week*
and the Festival of Marketing at Centaur Media Plc**

'Through The Marketing Academy I've worked with emerging marketing leaders and CMOs from the UK, the US and APAC for more than a decade and I can guarantee that *Boring2Brave* will provide a vital shot in the arm for anyone in B2B marketing who wishes to forge greater commercial success. In his book, Choueke shows how to harness one of the key things that exceptional marketers have in common: the raw bravery required to make impact and create change.'

Sherilyn Shackell, Founder and CEO, The Marketing Academy

'Mark captures perfectly the apathy that infects so much B2B marketing: the low levels of ambition, a lack of bold creative thinking and faltering self-belief. *Boring2Brave* is a much-needed rally cry to B2B marketers everywhere to stop being the brochure design department, stick their head above the parapet and have a go at REAL marketing. I intend to give this book to every client I work with.'

Simon McEvoy, UK Head of Strategy and UX at Omobono

BORING2
BRAVE

The 'bravery-as-a-strategy' mindset that's transforming B2B marketing

mark choueke

First published in Great Britain by Practical Inspiration Publishing, 2021

© Mark Choueke, 2021

The moral rights of the author have been asserted

ISBN   9781788602211 (print)
        9781788602204 (epub)
        9781788602198 (mobi)

Practical Inspiration
Publishing

MIX
Paper from
responsible sources
FSC
www.fsc.org   FSC® C013604

Contents

Author's note

My excellent publisher Alison Jones of Practical Inspiration Publishing warned me not to 'date' the book I hope you're about to enjoy.

However, when you're encouraging business people to be braver in a book you wrote in the midst of a global pandemic – one that sadly saw many of us lose loved ones while in the foothills of a potentially crushing recession – I feel compelled to mention it.

Not because Covid-19 informed a great deal of the content, but because the crisis it set in motion gave everybody the same platform and opportunity to be brave.

Indeed, every ounce of bravery one can conjure up during such exacting times stands to differentiate you from competitors, raise your profile and inspire others around you.

In times of uncertainty, 'bravery' ceases to be merely a lever to pull on if you feel so emboldened to chance the upper hand for your organisation. Rather, it often becomes the very key to survival and the defining difference among those who genuinely thrive amid disruption.

So, my apologies to my publisher. This is me risking dating the book from its very beginning.

I hope at least some of the content in *Boring2Brave* proves to remain relevant for years but in the short term, what was being experienced as I wrote it only strengthens the argument for finding inspiration in the stories I'm about to share.

I also have selfish reasons for wanting to mark the months in which I produced *Boring2Brave*. I write this in the final weeks of 2020. This year has at times been a blur, the same day repeated over and over; stuck at home finding reasons to remain positive and resilient. However, my particular Groundhog Day sensation was pricked by the tragedy of losing my dad.

I didn't see him for much of the four months before he died. He was shielding at home with Parkinson's and cancer. My mum used every ounce of courage and genius she possesses to keep him not just safe but happy.

Eventually, however, his condition deteriorated. When there was nothing more his doctors could do, his family finally went to be with him; to look after him, to be looked after by him, and to say goodbye.

So forgive me for dating Boring2Brave but I very much want to dedicate this book to mum and dad. Heroes both. A pair of English northerners with all the determination, decency, humour and grace so native to their Manchester and Liverpool roots but none of the swagger or brass so common to those cities. Instead, their currency was kindness. And in circumstances when kindness is the hardest thing to muster, it's the purest demonstration of bravery there is.

Preface

'Brave' is one of those notions you understand from the earliest memories of childhood.

I'm not referring to the way parents use the word when trying to soothe a toddler who's fallen over, or when calming a child before a simple medical procedure.

Instead, I'm talking about the instinctive respect bestowed upon the first kid in a gang to try a newly discovered, homemade swing across the river.

I'm referring to the badge of courage conferred upon the school student seen to talk back confidently to a bully in support of another.

Nothing need be discussed, agreed or voted on afterwards. Everyone walks away from such occurrences understanding the almost transactional nature of what happened – the peer in question just obtained 'leader' status in return for risks taken.

Context and specifics may differ as we grow, but the act of being uncommonly brave remains as rich. The thrill that comes with a single moment of audacity – a decision made and enacted in an instant – leaves a residue. What's left over is the knowledge you just redefined yourself, not just to others but also to yourself; the confidence that comes with a freshly discovered power to influence people and shape events.

Bravery is like a muscle. If flexed and practised regularly, it becomes a permanent and powerful addition to your skill-set. Unlike muscles though, bravery has a special characteristic. Bravery spreads.

The capacity you have (and you *do* have it) to challenge lazy conventions and destructive behaviours and to change things for the better inspires others around you to go ahead and do the same.

Unfortunately, the reverse is also true. Fearful, fainthearted and craven behaviour also spreads.

The preference for 'safety' – an aversion to risk – is a pernicious habit in B2B marketing and results in boring, ineffective work; work that fails to do the job marketing is supposed to do and that therefore smears the reputation of marketing as a discipline.

In B2B marketing, safety is a gamble. One that rarely pays off. Marketing is supposed to help your business grow. Quite simply, opting for safe, as opposed to brave, marketing can have the opposite effect.

A recent piece of research carried out by the B2B Institute and System1 revealed that 75% of B2B brands produce advertising that contributes zero long-term growth in market share.[1] Yet this is advertising, content, sponsorship or sales materials which the business owners pay handsomely to create.

Risk management is of course essential. We should continuously strive to identify potential risks, analyse them and take precautionary steps to protect against reputational or any other kind of harm. But being exposed to risks and taking risks are two different things.

Without the latter, we run identikit businesses and struggle to stand out. And without that standout, that brand awareness or any memorable, notable distinction, the execution of other necessary business functions – sales, contract renewals, hiring and so on – becomes materially more difficult.

Our organisations create processes and make business or product decisions entirely driven by eradicating all possible elements of risk. Yet these decisions make us ordinary and invisible. They prevent us from being competitive.

More than any other function or discipline, it's the responsibility of marketing to help our B2B organisations weigh up notions of safety and risk contextually. There shouldn't be any compromise on safety when it comes to public health or, say, aerospace engineering.

But consider instead the fields of art, music and sport, where those demonstrating audacity, adventure and daring are celebrated not just for their achievements but for their sheer spirit. More than merely 'loved', they are seen as *necessary* in their field for their capacity to smash through boundaries, drive progress and demonstrate what's possible.

---

[1] A. Rynne, 'Can powerful creative help businesses generate 20x more sales?' LinkedIn, 25 January 2021. Available from https://business.linkedin.com/marketing-solutions/blog/linkedin-b2b-marketing/2021/can-powerful-creative-help-businesses-generate-20x-more-sales- [accessed 6 March 2021].

Their peers who would fairly be characterised as typical, conventional or conservative (while perhaps qualified and proficient) don't reap the same goodwill. We care less about them. They become forgotten.

Marketing – by its very definition and purpose – should not be forgettable. It shouldn't leave people feeling indifferent.

Placing marketing in the same contextual sphere as aerospace engineering in terms of safety and risk is damaging. We should aim to make the target recipient of our marketing efforts feel *something* (or at least remember seeing it). It should be treated as a peer of art, or music, where the endeavour to play it safe and reduce risk is of less value than striving for the greater rewards reserved for the brave.

1 Is this book for you?

Here's a quick self-segmentation exercise. To save you potentially wasting time starting *Boring2Brave* at the expense of a better-suited and more relevant read, check to see if any of the following statements apply to your job in B2B marketing:

1   It's unlikely that the work you produced today will be valued, used or even remembered by anyone in your business 12 months from now.

2   You can't remember the last time you pitched an original and creative idea that your non-marketing colleagues embraced, built upon and used to drive significant growth.

3   You're bored. You enjoy being with your colleagues – maybe you're glad just to have a steady job – but your day-to-day work doesn't inspire or stretch you. There's little opportunity for you to stamp your personality or talent on what you produce.

If you relate to any one of these notions, you're not alone and this book is intended for you.

Years ago, when I was editor of *Marketing Week* magazine in London, I was chatting to one of the UK's most senior marketers. After a glittering career at a string of big consumer brands, he'd taken a job at a global technology brand that had both a B2B and a B2C arm. He was in charge of the B2B unit. Several months into the role, the veteran marketing director admitted to struggling.

'What's the problem?' I asked him.

'It's all so dry. Nobody wants to have any fun', he said. 'Consumer brands sell dreams. B2B brands sell safety. We sell conservation of a status quo and mitigation against the risk of our buyers losing their jobs.'

The marketing director felt that an organisation-wide suspicion of anything 'out of the ordinary' was preventing him from applying his skills to generate the sort of success he was accustomed to. Worse still, the company's wariness of doing things differently was preventing him from enjoying his work. He was miserable.

Today, what seemed a frustrating but 'immovable' truth a decade ago – that B2B marketing has to be dry, complex and boring – is thankfully no longer true.

Our industry's best are working without role models

Indeed, some practitioners aren't so willing to accept the status quo. Matthew Robinson has experienced a rapid rise to his current role of Contentsquare's senior marketing director for APAC. Robinson joined Contentsquare at the end of 2016 as head of marketing when the company was just a handful of people in Paris and London. Four years later, the digital experience analytics platform had raised a total of $312m in funding, was 600-people strong and serving 700 enterprise customers globally, including LVMH, Salesforce, Best Buy and American Express.

Robinson is a brilliant example of a modern B2B marketer: creative, technical and relentlessly focused on results that align with the wider business strategy.

But when looking for inspiration to inform his team's next campaign or activity – or even for role models to embolden and galvanise young marketers – Robinson says he's forced to look outside of B2B marketing.

'Most of our B2B marketing peers base everything they do on following and imitating poorly executed marketing they see done elsewhere by competitors.'

Is he disappointed in B2B marketing?

> One hundred per cent. I regularly find myself thinking: 'Where's the creativity? Who is there to look up to? Who are our role models supposed to be?' So yes, I'm disappointed but, at the same time, it's an opportunity to shine for those of us with a different approach.

Robinson is joined by many in having transformed his own trajectory and that of his organisation simply by refusing to be 'boring' and adopting 'brave'. To jolt a career into a higher gear and unearth fresh opportunities, B2B marketers need to view their role in a new light.

Taking charge of your own destiny and direction in the face of an organisational legacy isn't easy. The bravery to do so, in the face of enormous resistance, distinguishes those of us who succeed in both raising our own profile and driving up the value of our work from those that don't.

If you're sceptical that such a thing is even possible, again, you're not alone.

Mark Ritson spent 25 years working as a marketing professor at many of the world's top business schools. He's also worked as a global brand consultant for a client list that includes Subaru, Donna Karan, Westpac, Shiseido, Flight Centre, Johnson & Johnson, De Beers, and Sephora. For more than a decade he was also the in-house brand and marketing professor for LVMH, the world's largest luxury group.

To me though, Ritson is a friend and the incredible potty-mouthed star-columnist I poached from a competitor publication to come and write for me at *Marketing Week*. He now runs the *Marketing Week* mini-MBA courses he created, taken by thousands of marketers every year.

According to Ritson, the conventions and long-cemented beliefs around the role and value of B2B marketing make it extremely hard for any particular marketer to 'break with their programming': 'Many B2B marketers, even good ones, are in sales support roles and lack the institutional power to do anything better than what they're doing. They're effectively brochure design people, because that's what the organisation thinks marketing is.'

Much of the time, he adds, it's not the marketer's fault. 'If the structure of the organisation is so centred on sales, it's difficult for marketing to shout the odds for providing something more strategic.'

Ritson has a point. If company culture perceives each salesperson to be of equal worth to ten marketers, changing that mentality requires Herculean effort.

For marketers to instigate the difficult shift from being boring to brave in the name of better work is one thing. But how do we also achieve enough to significantly affect the perception of an ecosystem that doesn't respect what marketing is or does?

It is not for the fainthearted: patient and focused legwork (a series of actions with the onus all on you) is needed to build consensus in your organisation that marketing is a strategic driver of long-term growth.

I imagine it's what will stop a proportion of you from reading any further as you realise this book probably isn't for you. Ritson again: 'There are two things in question here. There's the current culture and expectations around B2B marketing, and then there's what the B2B marketer could deliver if expectations were raised.'

Ritson tells a story of being involved in a B2B company committed to improving and upgrading marketing:

> We trained everybody up and installed proper planning systems. We showed them zero-based budgeting and designed a proper strategy for each of their brands.

A third of the marketers left immediately of their own accord. Given the opportunity to do proper marketing, they were petrified.

Another third showed enthusiasm and tried their best but ultimately weren't capable.

And a third utterly thrived and took everything on board. That tells you a lot. There are people who don't want to be strategic or better at marketing. They like receiving a decent pay packet to do, essentially, promotional stuff.

What Ritson says may be true. But there are ways to increase our effectiveness and value as marketers and, while we're at it, how much we love and commit to our jobs.

That it will not be an easy ride should not deter us.

The average B2B marketing 'strategy' obsesses over channels – often crammed into a content calendar – but is bereft of any well-crafted segmentation, distinct positioning, stories or messaging.

Too few B2B marketers understand how to turn an 'e-book' into a manifesto. Scarcely any of us understand how or even why we'd build a solid business case to take to the CFO to argue the need to invest a hefty chunk of our budget on brand building. Few of us appreciate that, treated right, our brand actually stands to be our best sales tool, a powerful magnet for inbound leads.

A negligible number of the B2B marketers I've worked with found it easy to understand the transformational power of emotional messaging or that which can't easily be measured.

Your author and the men and women that contributed to this book believe B2B marketing no longer need be a subservient sales support function that receives little credit when things go right and much of the blame when they don't.

In Boring2Brave I've tried to:

★ uncover the series of fault lines that reduced B2B marketing's clout and effectiveness over time and break down the actions needed to reverse that shift;

★ detail how B2B marketers – regardless of their budget or seniority – earn the right to influence product development, pricing and other strategic business decisions;

★ point to case studies, research and personal stories that demonstrate the raw commercial value of creativity in B2B marketing and outline strategies for achieving internal buy-in when employing it;

★ draw lessons from a string of candid, original interviews with leaders on how they grew their influence, boosted their impact and raised their profile.

If you're excited – or even sceptical but up for a few good yarns from elsewhere in B2B marketing – read on.

2 Bravery: The ultimate leadership development training

Two things separate us from machines and animals: we have ideas and see those ideas as an opportunity to break from our 'programming' if we think we can improve things.

Throughout my career, nothing has challenged my belief that being brave is the surest way of achieving commercial success and, more importantly, personal happiness and peace of mind.

My contention that 'being brave = successful business' will be explored in these pages but beforehand, here are two more things to know about bravery.

Firstly and quite simply, it's easy to be brave. Anyone can do it.

Secondly and far less simply, few others in B2B marketing *are* doing it.

Some questions: Do you feel too smart for your current job? Are you nagged by the feeling most days that you could be offering so much more? And do you reckon it's just you feeling that way?

Does it feel like you're fulfilling your incredible potential as a B2B marketer?

Look around you. How many others in B2B marketing do you see doing anything groundbreaking, or even just fun?

A moment to define 'brave'

The *Cambridge Dictionary* defines brave as 'showing no fear of dangerous or difficult things', while the *Oxford English Dictionary* defines it as 'ready to face and endure danger or pain; showing courage'. *Collins*, meanwhile, offers its definition as 'having or displaying courage, resolution or daring; not cowardly or timid'.[2]

These are ok, I guess.

I'd add something to the definition of brave to capture an important element. The first parts of all those definitions are fine – let's blend them to get a decent version... 'ready to display courage, resolution or daring...'

The ingredient I'd add is simply: '...for the better'.

Bravery is how we improve things: change a situation for the better. Why else would you bother being brave? As the Cambridge and Oxford dictionaries both make perfectly clear, being brave means enduring difficulty and pain. Who needs that? Nobody. Not unless you're going to improve your position or environment – or, if you're *really* brave, that of others.

Consider any historical figure we celebrate for bravery. Were any of them ever trying to do anything else but change something bad into something good?

Day-to-day opportunities to be brave as a B2B marketer

In a work scenario, brave can mean any number of things. Sometimes it is just raising the awkward question everyone recognises needs asking but which has so far been resolutely ignored. Other times being brave is challenging an established and trusted process that repeatedly produces mediocre results.

And although bravery almost always results in 'better', the organisation isn't the key beneficiary of you being brave. Brave is an investment – one that comes with calculated risk – where the ROI is principally felt by you.

---

[2] Definitions of 'brave': *Cambridge Dictionary*. Available from https://dictionary.cambridge.org/dictionary/english/brave; *Oxford English Dictionary*. Available from: www.lexico.com/definition/brave; *Collins English Thesaurus*. Available from www.collinsdictionary.com/dictionary/english-thesaurus/brave [accessed 6 March 2021].

With every brave moment you gain influence, respect, personal agency, confidence, admirers, listeners, followers and fans. You build a reputation for leadership and therefore increase your chance of being promoted into roles that require you to lead.

The best part, however, is your effect on others around you. With every flash of bravery you successfully execute (not all of them will go well – sometimes being brave means accepting when something you tried didn't work), you pass on permission to be brave to your peers.

Three things that characterise acts of business bravery:

1 They go against the grain: they typically challenge a powerful, prevailing wisdom and therefore feel risky and uncomfortable.

2 Something is improved; bravery is used to unlock a bad situation or advance a good one.

3 You feel a surge, a thrill, as you carry out your act of bravery; you're left afterwards feeling vital and like you could do it again immediately – like the electric buzz that comes immediately after a 10K run (experienced by this author just the once so far...).

Why Boring2Brave?

I'm in B2B technology marketing, which should be one of the best, most exciting occupations in the world. You'd expect this particular discipline to be moving, innovating and experimenting at the same breathless pace as the products we promote. And in the absence of much true brand differentiation across much of the B2B tech market, there should be daily excitement within thousands of smart companies about the chance to exploit brilliant, emotion-led campaigns that capture both share of voice and share of market.

Instead, B2B tech marketers have to work hard to avoid an existence of producing boring, technical and largely ineffective work, to demand.

Before my current role – I'm the marketing director for leading customer referral platform Mention Me – I was an external marketing consultant working globally for in the B2B tech space. The stuff many of us create in the name of driving growth (the white papers, the e-books, the webinars) doesn't just bore the very targets we're trying to impress; many of us are boring ourselves.

So, for all of the hope I have about sparking a conversation that might improve B2B marketing's impact, influence and fortunes, I'm just as interested in seeing if we can unshackle ourselves from the humdrum, often joyless, task that currently is so much B2B marketing.

I believe B2B marketing could create bigger, better, braver stories for prospects and customers, forged from creativity, craft and even audacity in the name of long-term brand building.

There is untold commercial opportunity for any business or brand that takes this challenge to heart.

Mostly though, the stories and case studies gathered and shared here come with the conviction that B2B marketers can not only boost the perception of the value of marketing but at the same time increase their own personal leadership profile, influence and financial worth.

Just by being brave.

3 Step 1: The decision

So, what's our first move? I think it's a conscious decision on our part as B2B marketers to no longer be a second-class business function. Let's simply decide to stop being the punchline.

Compared with the sales, product or engineering teams, the marketing function doesn't always command a lot of respect across many B2B organisations.

We need to change that. *We* do. Nobody else.

Some years back, I was standing among my new colleagues in a Monday morning 'all-hands' company meeting, shortly after taking up a global marketing role for a thriving B2B scale-up SaaS business.

Towards the end of the meeting, the COO was highlighting a few vacancies we were looking to fill across various teams and asking us all to be active recruiters from within our networks. He also encouraged us to think about these vacancies as opportunities for advancing our own careers, advising us to think about how we could broaden our skills and development by switching from one team to another.

'We've hired you already,' he said. 'We believe you're the right people to grow this business. It matters less to us *how* you contribute to that growth. If you wanted to explore a jump from say, customer success to marketing, we'd love to help.'

A roar of laughter erupted and didn't die down quickly. I didn't immediately pick up that the notion being mocked was that anyone would *choose* to join the marketing team, or indeed that there was anything particularly vicious about what seemed good-natured banter.

In the marketing meeting immediately afterwards, however, my young colleagues felt stung. 'That's exactly how marketing is seen,' they told me.

I was feeling good about my new job so wasn't ready to buy in to what I thought seemed a collective inferiority complex. But over the next few weeks I saw they were right. It wasn't even a secret. Some of the most visible, vocal and celebrated 'rock stars' of the product, engineering and sales teams felt entirely permitted to talk down to marketing in a way that was unpleasant, let alone unprofessional.

Elevating the profile and reputation of marketing's work and demonstrating its role in the company's success became every bit as important to me over the next three years as driving growth externally.

Sadly, *demanding* respect doesn't work any more than *begging* for respect does. So, we needed to earn it and we did.

Good news alert: You're the solution to your own problem

As marketers we are the only solution to this problem. It's only us and our teams that can change the perception of marketing.

Doug Kessler, creative director and founder of crack B2B marketing agency Velocity Partners, started his career working on consumer brands for advertising agency Ogilvy & Mather in New York City before switching to his first love, B2B.

> For most of my career in B2B, marketing had very little respect and actually didn't deserve it. There wasn't a lot to respect. That's changing fast. We're finding some fantastic marketing-driven B2B companies who are winning specifically because the marketing team is taking itself more seriously.

Taking yourself 'more seriously' is a difficult thing to do within an embedded culture that has long established your value as a lesser function of the organisation. But that's only the case for as long as you accept it as the truth.

Once you've made the decision that you're only going to produce brilliant and effective marketing almost regardless of what else you're asked to deliver – the kind of marketing that drives growth by an order of magnitude *and* makes a company famous – the outcomes are understood by everyone.

Very few of your colleagues (or even members of the management) understand the necessary inputs of superlative marketing like you do. Everybody, however, recognises success.

That's the good news. The less good news is that unless you're lucky enough to already have demonstrable success to show why you deserve the trust and time to build the foundations of long-term growth, you'll meet with scrutiny and suspicion.

There are plenty of resources online that provide strategies for having more business-like conversations with other stakeholders to help them understand the value of marketing done well.

I've written about many of these resources on the blog on my Boring2Brave.com website and believe we should gather round such tools. The key resource that this chapter is concerned with, however, is your own personal human resource.

The path of 'least resistance' turns out to be far from the easiest journey

One of the clients we partnered at Rebeltech, the B2B tech marketing agency I founded with Nicole Lyons in 2017, had a pretty good product. The client also had a handful of high-profile customers through which they could demonstrate some credible use cases.

The client paid well. It made sense then that my partner Nic, now head of marketing at B2B marketplace Axora, and I were both very personally involved in the account. Our weekly meetings with the client were attended by the CEO and founder, a non-executive director, the sales director and the head of marketing.

The marketer didn't speak in these meetings. He offered no opinion or contribution whatsoever. Uncomfortably, he was regularly the butt of his colleagues' jokes – jokes made with Nic, me and our team in the room.

We tried hard to engage him and show him support. We knew though that we'd have little to do with him directly when marketing decisions were being made. If we needed approval for anything, it would come from the non-exec director. If we wanted to build some pre-meeting support for an idea, we'd speak to the founder.

The marketing guy would come to the lobby to let us in the client's building and he'd show us back down to the door on the way out. Besides that, he never sought a private conversation with us regarding the work or demanded any of our time for himself.

He was responsible for tracking digital marketing channels. As far as he was concerned, his world and our world – strategic growth initiatives, content creation, brand campaigns and PR – did not overlap.

When we quietly asked him how he felt about the way he was treated, he would smile and shrug. 'They don't understand what I do, how we get people to the website, so I just carry on.'

The marketer once told us that the sales team and non-exec director had him regularly spending entire days stuffing padded envelopes with soft, cuddly toys and sending them to prospects for their children. We once saw him doing it – Nicole and I were passing a room at our client's office and caught sight of him through an open door so popped in to say hello. There was a pile of the soft toys the size of an SUV. The stack of envelopes was nearly as large.

This guy wasn't a junior or an intern. He was in his late 30s. And he was no dunce. He was smart, skilled and, incidentally, lovely too. I was constantly baffled as to why he didn't do more to alter his situation.

Nic, my Rebeltech co-founder and our CEO, has a personal take on it:

> These so-called marketing roles exist everywhere. I've been in that situation where you're supposedly responsible for marketing but treated as a dogsbody because someone hired marketers without really ever understanding what marketing is.
>
> Everything that doesn't fall into anyone else's direct remit is handed to 'marketing'.
>
> So instead of being known by your colleagues for leading the drive for growth, they know you as the person who organises the summer and Christmas parties.
>
> At events you're expected to stand at the door greeting guests and handing out name badges. I remember a number of occasions during my early career being asked five minutes before a meeting – a meeting I felt I should have been in but wasn't invited to – to print off and compile the documents for the meeting or take coffee orders.

Nicole says she's quit jobs that came with a working environment or mistaken perception of marketing that she found she simply couldn't change for the better.

> I think you get two different kinds of people. Those that will stand for it; maybe it bothers them and maybe it doesn't, but they rationalise it because they're generally happy or are well paid and therefore comfortable. And then you get people who, regardless of their salary, know they can't stay.

Our client's marketer never felt it was his right to turn to his colleagues and say: 'Hey, I don't need you in this meeting with Rebeltech. I've got some ideas for a programme of activities I'd like them to work on for us.' He never demanded the marketing job. So we answered to others. We worked for people who neither understood nor fully trusted marketing.

It's time for us to decide how much influence we want.

4 Step 2: The doing (while we do, we also need to teach)

Two audiences within B2B organisations need to better understand marketing and drive more success from it.

The first is us – the marketers. As relentless as it sounds, we can't afford to stop trying to understand the potential for producing better, more effective work and earning our right to do it.

The second audience that needs a clearer understanding of marketing and how to make it work is our colleagues.

Check out any B2B marketing role being advertised right now, particularly in the B2B tech space. Go and look at the jobs page on LinkedIn or similar, right now.

Read any of those job descriptions and the accompanying skills requirements and you'd be forgiven for wondering whether they actually want to hire someone gifted – someone with your tremendous and diverse skill-set and experience. Or do they just want a body, a compliant robot that will fit what seems an industry-standard template of a marketing programme they've already decided they need?

Digital marketing is heavily emphasised along with any other current marketing trends or buzzwords, regardless of what marketing needs to achieve for the hiring business. Even for senior roles (with an assumed value placed on strategic capability), many hiring processes suggest that if a candidate has a pulse and is willing to manage a monthly menu of one webinar, four email 'campaigns', ongoing PPC and SEO activity and any other lead generation or digital acquisition tactics they remember to name in the interview, then that applicant will be perfect. In short, most job ads scream that they've been written by someone without a nanobyte of true marketing experience or understanding to their name.

When we start in new jobs, we tend to accept this outsider's narrow view of marketing's role and capability and behave accordingly, rather than adopt the role of credible expert – there to educate the organisation from within.

Is marketing harder than engineering?

Marketing is so much more complex and powerful than they – and sometimes we – give it credit for.

The hierarchy of B2B companies and B2B tech companies prioritises sales and engineering, respectively.

Imagine for a moment the fire hose of mockery you'd face if you dared suggest in your organisation that marketing is more difficult than engineering. Because it shouldn't be, right? Marketing absolutely shouldn't be harder than engineering. Capturing people's attention should be easier than building a brilliant product or technology.

But as chief Martech blogger and HubSpot's VP Platform Ecosystem Scott Brinker points out, of all the various challenges a business faces, 'the software is often the easy bit'. Brinker cites the job of going to market with a decent narrative as 'the really hard part – the bottleneck'.

It's a counterintuitive thought, even for me as a marketer. Getting yourself seen and heard in the right way feels like it should be straightforward. But instead we, as B2B, accept such poor marketing outcomes that you could reasonably interpret it as B2B having a wilful disinterest in marketing.

The truth is that while marketing understands at least the basic rudiments of the other disciplines such as sales, finance, operations and so on, somehow otherwise great business people are born or made without any interest in learning marketing at all.

Good businesses are, by their nature, polymaths. They operate around the effective integration and mutually beneficial relationships of multiple disparate disciplines, skills, activities and perspectives.

Weirdly, most businesses ignore that truth and instead require every strand of an organisation to fall into what Rory Sutherland cites as a singularly left-brained culture.

Sutherland, vice chairman at Ogilvy UK, regular TED speaker on the business value of behavioural psychology and author of *Alchemy: The Surprising Power of Ideas That Don't Make Sense*, bemoans the view that logical, numerical and economic perspectives so often dominate at the expense of creative solutions to problems.

He argues that marketing is indeed more difficult than other more dominant B2B organisational functions such as sales and engineering:

> What engineers don't see is that their coding problems are well-defined and that, as with much of the scientific realm, there's a single best answer. That's simply not true of the problems that good marketers solve where dilemmas can only be answered subjectively.
>
> Engineering and finance and economics are all effectively a branch of physics where there's a single right answer and every problem is one of optimisation. In physics, the opposite of a good idea is wrong. Marketing is a psychological area of activity where there isn't a single right answer and where the opposite of a good idea can be another good idea.

If Sutherland is correct, it not only takes a different type of brain to skilfully negotiate marketing problems than it does the more rational, logical disciplines, it also arguably requires a braver soul. Faced with unlimited options for 'the right answer', one needs a stronger conviction to develop and pitch a 'best next move' in a specific direction than if there was only one good answer to choose from.

We need to develop the language with which we explain why this alternative, 'right-brained' mode of problem solving is as vital as the logic and order that underpins the other departments and functions.

It's what makes marketing unique and incredibly valuable to the world's best businesses that employ it so well.

We should stop hiding silently behind our classroom desks and come up to the front to teach our peers how the things we do can trigger so much value.

5 When you think you're Han Solo but you're actually C-3PO

Ask any human being of a certain age who, given the choice of C-3PO and Han Solo, they relate to more.

Ask which one of the pair they'd prefer to be likened to.

You already know the answer, right? It's the sexy, wise-cracking guy with a blaster that somehow makes a waistcoat and jodhpurs look cool.

And yet many B2B marketers actively choose to be C-3PO as soon as they enter their workspaces.

In case you're struggling to remember, or have never seen the original Star Wars movies (in which case close this book right now because you've got more important things to do), C-3PO is the shiny, gold robot who talks like, well, a robot. His appearance is flawless and polished, his manner pointlessly formal and subservient.

C-3PO has a thing for using technical, complex language and is hugely risk averse. In short, C-3PO is B2B marketing.

If C-3PO had a LinkedIn profile it would read something like this:

> First-class droid, skilled in physical, mathematical and medical sciences, and programmed for etiquette and protocol.
>
> Fluent in more than six-million forms of communication and comfortable with high technical complexity.
>
> Built by Jedi Anakin Skywalker but also has served Princess Leia Organa and Luke Skywalker at senior level as well as numerous others across the Resistance.

Awesome podcast guest with an inspirational story, global interstellar experience and a powerful network.

While we B2B marketers inadvertently resemble C-3PO with our addiction to corporate and technical jargon, perfectly shiny appearance, religious faith in logic, and boring, scaredy-cat approach, we actively snub everything we love about Han Solo. In fact, we show nothing but contempt for the characteristics we admire in Captain Solo.

'Use the ~~force~~ flaws...'

What makes Han Solo a fierce leader of the Rebel Alliance are the same things that make him the opposite of C-3PO. He's flawed. He's scrappy. He's cocky. He has a tendency to act on instinct in the absence of a plan. He refuses to bow to anyone but also has loyalty to friends and a commitment to doing the 'real' right thing as opposed to the 'logically' right thing. And he shows bravery.

If we're looking at substance over style, the main thing that separates Han Solo from C-3PO is that Han is prepared to take a risk.

C-3PO is a pessimist who fears the worst. He has a weird fetish for oversharing to anyone in the room the improbability of success and indeed the likelihood of a horrible death in the next few space-minutes.

All the other characters involved in the Rebellion believe in hope and optimism, including R2-D2, C-3PO's best friend and fellow droid. So if you're wondering whether this is just me indulging in a rather nasty strain of 'droid-ism', it isn't.

In fact, if for any reason R2-D2 were seeking an alternative career, he would make a far more effective B2B marketer than C-3PO. R2-D2 combines unrivalled data expertise with creativity and, perhaps most importantly, bare-faced cheek.

I'll bet C-3PO *loves* thought leadership white papers. Unnecessarily long white paper introductions, full of complex words and phrases – that then in turn necessitate a glossary to explain those words – are, I don't doubt, among C-3PO's favourite things.

R2-D2 would not, I suspect, enjoy thought leadership white papers. Han Solo definitely wouldn't. He probably doesn't check his emails regularly enough to find them pitched in his inbox but even if he did, he wouldn't download them and absolutely wouldn't read them.

Do you sound like a droid?

I estimate there's a million blogs and other pieces of content urging you to make your business sound more 'human'. I'm sure I agree with many of them. But even after we've read these blogs and nodded sagely, there's the small matter of how we do that and who decides on our tone of voice.

Have a look at your content, your sales collateral, your email campaign subject headers, your sign-offs, your social media posts and ask yourself: 'Do I sound like a person or a droid?'

'Am I allowing myself to be funny or irreverent... even scrappy?'

As a first step, think about why you love Han Solo or, for that matter, why people like each other.

Why do we love funny people? What is it about the making of an instinctive, spur-of-the-moment joke that makes people feel so alive and engaged?

It's part of the same reason we love blooper-reels from our favourite shows and movies.

Sometimes coming off as real, maybe even making a mistake but bringing everyone in on the joke, makes for better content than always sounding perfect and polished.

Approaching your marketing in C-3PO mode means the majority of your target prospects and customers will remain blind to your messaging and copy. You're not giving them a single match with which to spark any excitement.

You want proof? How many of you have posted something like this onto social media?

> Excited to be hosting this exclusive webinar/panel/fireside chat aimed at showcasing how today's most forward-looking businesses are capitalising on the latest trends to elevate and maximise their opportunities in tomorrow's marketplace by utilising 'next-generation' frictionless data solutions.

Any idea what this session is all about or how you might survive it if you were sitting in the front row and couldn't leave early?

No.

Me neither.

Not just a B2B thing

By the way, accidentally being C-3PO isn't just a B2B thing. B2C companies sometimes unintentionally choose to be C-3PO rather than Han Solo too. Check out this incredible job description attached to a vacancy at Unilever (thanks to copywriter extraordinaire 'Wordman' Dave Harland for directing me to this):

MAIN JOB PURPOSE:

The Enterprise UX Assistant Manager is a member of the Packaging Excellence Team (within the Packaging Capability) and reports to the Digital Experience Change Leader. The purpose of the UX Designer is, to establish user experience design practices for Packaging's internal digital tool development through applying collaborative design techniques and user/client centred communication approaches. This will help deliver valuable, usable, appealing and engaging digital enterprise user experiences underpinning the strategy to Disrupt through Digital.[3]

How much do you love that? Clearly written by someone who's bigly into SEO. Read it again one more time and hover for a moment to luxuriate in its glorious gibberish.

I adore that the Packaging 'Excellence' team sits within the Packaging 'Capability' team.

'Rob, you've done it. You're joining the Excellence team…the packaging elite.'

'Great, who do I report to?'

'You'll report into the head of "merely capable."'

Impressed with the pure 'C-3PO-ness' of the job description, I went looking for the job application form. If you've got the appetite for more – or you just want to feel better about the copy of the last job ad you published on LinkedIn – cast your eyes on the instructions for applying for this role:

Please note: As part of the job application, you will be asked to complete a brief online application form. Completion of the form is required in order to be considered. Please allow yourself enough time to complete the application form as when filled out partially or not at all it may adversely affect the progress of your application. Please be aware that you will have to complete the form at once as you will be unable to return to it later.

I mean… wow. Just, wow.

There's a form to fill in to get the job. You know, like an application form. Only, you should have it under advisement that the form is necessary if you want to be considered, so definitely fill that thing in. With your details. But – and here's the big 'but' – if you DON'T fill it in, we won't

---

[3] Job description available from www.wizbii.com/company/unilever/job/ ux-designer-204 [accessed 6 March 2021].

actually be able to consider you for the job. Because the two things are connected. And when you fill it in? Well, you'll need time – time to do it. Because that's the other thing we didn't tell you yet – actually filling it in will take you some... time. And fill it in fully too. Don't go missing important bits out because then... then it wouldn't be 'filling the form in'; it would be like, 'not quite filling ALL the form in'... and that's no good either... Etc.

You get my point. Many of us are wasting a lot of time sounding like a Star Wars character that, at best, we all felt a bit sorry for.

We should start sounding like the character everybody gravitated to, the one everybody listened to, the one we all wanted to be.

6   How much do you spend to be invisible?

Many B2B tech startups resent having to spend large budgets on marketing because it never seems to work for them.

There's a good reason for this lack of success. B2B companies often work hard but not very intelligently on marketing and end up spending all their money on being quietly invisible. Their marketing budget is all geared towards generating and progressing individual leads and closing deals.

You can count on one hand the enterprise technology startups that have spent their budget establishing a unique positioning, building a brand and making it famous through the brilliant telling of big stories. A clue: they're the very successful ones we've all heard of.

Without those elements: the brand, the positioning, the stories and the fame, you've got no marketing. What you've got are channels. The website, the investment into SEO and paid search, the exhibition stall, the webinar, the e-book series, the paid social strategy, the blog. The PR. These are all just channels.

The 'sexy product, dull marketing' disconnect

It's surprising how often visionary startups that have built a beautiful technology, that compete in the race for top talent and hire the smartest people to drive superb customer success programmes, are then happy to go to market with such tepid marketing.

There's a real disconnect. B2B tech startup founders are typically smart, passionate and utterly obsessive and detail-focused people.

Why would you work so bloody hard and make so many personal sacrifices to invest in creating such a world-class company and product, but then let your marketing be so bland? Your marketing! The bit that you want your customers to notice and how others learn about you... why would you allow that bit of your company to be mediocre?

'A lot of it is just about people not knowing how stuff works,' Doug Kessler, the Velocity Partners founder, tells me.

> They don't study marketing. We study this stuff. It's clear to us what's good and bad but for most people, they just know they need to 'do' marketing and when they have to do something they've never done before, they do the obvious thing: they look at what others have done.

> If you're going to build a bookshelf, you look at another bookshelf and go, 'yeah, make it like that'. And you're not even aiming for great. You're just aiming for something that passes for a bookshelf. And it's true with marketing too.

The enemy of brave marketing isn't disastrous marketing, notes Kessler, it's mediocre marketing.

> It's not the big flops that get me cross. The opposite of brave marketing is not the massive 'tone-deaf' fail, like the Windows 7 Party idea. Yes, that was a huge fail but that's not the enemy – they tried something different and it flopped. The enemy of brave is mediocrity or not even trying.

Kessler has a point. How many content marketing briefs have you seen that said: 'we want you to take all the time and energy needed for this to be the best piece on this topic ever published?'

Instead, many B2B marketing 'strategies' forget to define the content altogether. They neglect to determine the themes and topics, the distinct point of view, the things they want to take a particular stance on that will carve them out a memorable position in the market and differentiate them from competitors.

Case study: The Future of Travel

Matthew Robinson, APAC marketing director for digital experience analytics leader Contentsquare, has built his reputation on brave ideas, energy and creativity.

His pet hate, he shares, is seeing brilliant ideas 'clipped, trimmed and stifled' until they've lost everything that made them so potent and exciting in the first place.

> It happens constantly in B2B. You pitch an idea which knocks everyone's socks off but then your superior starts 'spreadsheeting' it. Launch is put on hold, to be scheduled

only after you've written the copy for every communication – every social post, every blog, every notification – that you plan to release over the three-month campaign. Every word requires sign-off along with the 'A' and 'B' test version for every headline and email subject header.

Sometimes mapping out every detail of a big idea for multiple internal presentations and committee scrutiny, before it's even out in the world, kills the idea before it's born.

I believe in planning for quality and originality. But with that, there's also something to be said for 'let's get this out the door – let's launch it and respond to the reaction we receive'. Yes, there will be mistakes and necessary tweaks but for me, that's preferable to the particular sort of 'innovation death march' that we're so good at in B2B.

In Robinson's view, what we do to prune and shear big ideas in B2B is less about safety and more about fear.

I wouldn't be surprised if good ideas get stifled in B2B probably more than in any other industry or sector.

In Robinson's view, the only two things that can impact the 'safety status quo' in a specific organisation are if a direct competitor does something outlandishly brave or eye-catching and reaps the success.

Believe me, that's when you'd see bosses scrambling to replicate bravery pretty bloody quickly – or if a marketer decides to go 'rogue'.

Robinson recalls one campaign in a previous job where he decided he wasn't going to wait for a consensus to mow his idea to 'tidy perfection'. At the time, he was product marketing manager for the travel industry for SaaS customer experience and personalisation software Qubit.

I came up with a campaign called The Future of Travel. It had nothing to do directly with Qubit's product. It was about imagining what travel will look like 20 years from now and what changes the digital passenger experience might entail between now and then.

I got futurists and technologists as well as travel industry execs involved. It was really cool. I was nervous though that we were going to kill it with a ton of 'Five ways travel brands can optimise their personalisation strategies' type materials. I wanted images of astronauts in rockets next to Wilbur and Orville Wright on their first successful flight. I wanted to highlight the milestones of travel that we've already achieved and start a conversation with the industry on what we might achieve next.

We launched it quickly and I did everything I could to avoid the box-ticking exercise. I didn't know how it would go, but actually seeing it work so well was a bit of an awakening to me. We did a mail-out of a book that was pure editorial content – free of product.

It was well received so we followed it up with an event which we hosted at RSA House in Mayfair, London. The place has a room with a domed glass ceiling that illuminates a series of paintings including *The Progress of Human Knowledge* by James Barry. It was all very apt.

Our guest speakers were incredible and created a real sense of a movement. It was a 'big-thinking', inspiring campaign that was repeated and expanded in subsequent years.

I was chatting to my travel industry sales colleague after that first campaign who told me he signed over a million dollars of new business based purely on that campaign. That was hugely successful for us. And it wasn't because it was an amazingly detailed, mapped out campaign. It was just a cool, creative idea that resonated. I was probably lucky to get away with doing it without all the normal 'checks and balances' and planning meetings but it worked. That was when I first learned to be 'me' as a marketer and trust in my instincts. I'm totally up for having a plan but I'll avoid over-planning when I think great ideas are at risk.

***

The far too well-trodden path into marketing for most tech startups (and many larger, more mature organisations are equally guilty of this) is to completely ignore the crucial 'what's our story, what do we have the right to talk about that's interesting, what's the turf we can uniquely own that speaks to us and none of our competitors?' stage of building a marketing strategy.

Instead, they jump straight to the tactics and look to hire themselves some expertise in their chosen media channel – events, content and most commonly digital marketing.

In many ways this is fine. Digital marketing is a phenomenally powerful and targeted way of getting your message out. The thing though about digital marketing is that it was never supposed to be a replacement for a whole bunch of channels and activities that (weirdly) often get clustered together and labelled 'traditional' marketing. Digital wasn't supposed to be a replacement or an alternative to events, advertising or PR; it was supposed to be an amazing and complementary addition.

Digital marketing channels are just that – a set of channels. A vehicle for your message. You can target your prospects with as much laser-focus that today's technology permits you but if you don't hit them in the brain, the heart or the gut with an appeal or urgency, they'll remain blind to your efforts.

The marketing metrics you need to keep to yourself

It can be exhausting watching marketers in meetings, reporting back on progress in metrics that mean little to anyone else in the room.

Some digital marketing metrics are really important to share with colleagues from other functions but most shouldn't be talked about anywhere else than in marketing team meetings. Sure, this week's uplifts in engagement metrics and website visitors are things to celebrate internally among the team – they show you're doing some of the right things.

But those of us who stuff our reports with these metrics for the board or management team are often the same ones wondering why B2B marketing isn't respected.

Andrew Logan founded Floww Digital, a full-service digital marketing agency based in Scotland that's serving clients the world over. Floww is so good because Andrew and his team understand that 'sales pay the rent; likes and shares don't':

I think that particularly with digital stuff you can end up down a rabbit hole of speaking a language nobody cares about or even understands.

We all need to understand we're not digital marketers. We're marketers that have valuable digital skills. But what we do is marketing. We're here to communicate an idea. Trying to do that without the great copy and brand-building stuff and the trust those things generate? Well, nobody will buy you.

The delivery channels aren't where you get to be brave in your marketing, states Logan – it's the messaging that plays that part:

Marketing is an expensive waste of time if you can't tell a useful or entertaining story; if you're not prepared to take the risk needed to stand out.

Marketers have heard people tell them 'we need content' and they've misinterpreted it as needing to create volumes of content, regardless of quality. They churn it out with no distinguishable tone of voice and it goes unseen and unheard.

Author and marketing consultant Peter Field, who along with Les Binet has for decades produced the definitive body of work on what makes for marketing effectiveness, told me not long ago about a meeting he was invited to attend with a tech startup. The business wanted to explore how it could up its game in marketing. Field asked the senior management to tell him about the company's brand.

'Total silence,' he remembers. 'They had never thought about brand.'

My advice to them was, look, before you even think about a communications plan, think about what your brand is. Go, do the basic homework. It was absolutely astonishing. Page one stuff.

Field's experience is not unusual. I've consulted for many potentially great businesses that were struggling for awareness but at the same time refuted with almost disgust any reference to them as a 'brand'. 'Tech start-ups', says Field, 'are started and populated by people on the nerd spectrum, some of whom have a visceral dislike of marketing.'

They think if you have to advertise then you've failed. That advertising is 'so last millennium'. That growth can be done using big data and digital, and serving our messages, using data and trying to be relevant. Then when they get to a certain size and they've run out of people 'they already know' to sell to, the growth dries up and they realise the benefits of advertising.

Field's frustration is with people that don't understand marketing yet have it in their remit to direct the people that 'own' and execute marketing.

As per the previous chapter, it's our responsibility as marketers to gather the data, case studies and all other evidence required to push back. It's our responsibility to teach, not to blindly obey.

If we spend our organisations' money helping them become invisible, we can't be surprised when we ourselves become invisible within our organisations; when nobody actively seeks us out or asks for time in our calendars to help influence the next big growth idea.

7   'Different' is your job…

An under-discussed problem in marketing is that nearly half of brands are today mistaken for their competitors. In other words, most marketing today triggers buyers to purchase a competitive brand, not the brand doing the marketing.

Jon Lombardo, global lead, The B2B Institute[4]

The tyranny of 'best practice'

One of my favourite first-page introductions of any business book out there is that in *Zero to One* by Peter Thiel. 'Today's best practices lead to dead ends; the best paths are new and untried,' Thiel writes.[5] The Paypal co-founder states that the single most powerful pattern he's tracked in 'successful' people is that they find value in unexpected places by thinking about business from first principles instead of formulas.

Formulas for business success shouldn't exist. How does anyone expect to copy another company and attain the same success, without the same people?

The problem with best practice is it stops you having to think. It prevents you from looking a bit harder and considering all the angles of a problem or opportunity.

---

[4] J. Lombardo, 'The science of brand'. LinkedIn. Available from https://business.linkedin.com/marketing-solutions/content-marketing/b2b-trends-services/the-science-of-brand [accessed 6 March 2021].
[5] P. Thiel with B. Masters, *Zero to One*. Virgin Books, 2014, Preface.

Of course, we should look to templatise certain processes. It means we can scale. The people that need to look for templates and repeatable, scalable processes, though, are operations directors. That's their job.

It's not the job of the marketer. What marketers should templatise and scale is a culture of freedom, innovation, 'test and learn'. We should be gently pushing back at templates wherever possible in favour of creative, innovative thinking that stands to get us an advantage if only because nobody else could possibly have imagined our solution.

Unleash your inner B2B hero

We're marketing. Our job is to help our company and product stand out. To differentiate. To be remembered.

If our brand, product or message isn't memorable, we'll not reach or sell to new customers and our organisations can't grow.

Our remit, then, is literally to be different. We get paid to ensure our organisations don't blend in. That's hard. And because it often means taking risks, doing stuff nobody's tried before and that might not work, it requires bravery.

It's the job. Being brave is the job. Not many of us are doing it. Because being brave is scary.

If you're not being brave at work, it might be because you don't know how to start. Here's how – according to Olympic gold medallist Seb Coe (strangely, he used to be one of my bosses):

'Use the energy fear creates.'

What does that mean? It means that when you do something as scary as leave your comfort zone and risk trying something new, you're going to have to do 'something' with the feeling of terror you feel. You can either let it consume you into bluster, clumsiness and underperformance or use it to drive you to a 'win'. Use that energy to do something, change something, fix something no one knew was broken.

Don't let having a marketing function in your business become someone's choice

All this might sound unscientific but we're approaching a point where companies might start asking themselves why they have a marketing function in the business at all.

In February 2020, Australian marketing intelligence analysis website MI3 commented on a survey conducted in the *Financial Times* that it said 'should seriously worry marketers'. The survey found that the vast majority of business leaders have lost faith in brand and its power to drive growth. Meanwhile, it continued, 'B2B marketers have painted themselves into a corner by focusing on short-term sales metrics. They're so tactical they don't have time to think about brand, let alone long-term strategy.'[6]

Because we build and operate businesses around what Rory Sutherland described earlier in these pages as 'left-brained' beliefs and procedures, we're trained to believe any process that cuts cost is good; even if the saving means we buy suboptimal talent and tools.

The LinkedIn B2B Institute's Jann Schwarz, a former WPP exec before joining LinkedIn, thinks that both brands and agencies have confused efficiency with effectiveness:

> You can be extremely efficient at being useless as a marketing organisation. You can be incredibly effective as a marketing organisation without being very efficient.

> Effectiveness should come first. Efficiency is a nice thing and you should strive for it. But efficiency for the sake of efficiency is a terrible, terrible way to live.

Efficiency in B2B marketing currently trumps all other arguments and approaches. Pursuing efficiency though leaves no room for the magic that makes for great, memorable and effective marketing. Because efficiency can be predicted, scaled and measured, and magic can't.

The costs of making magical and memorable marketing can't be easily forecast; nor can the success it drives be easily guaranteed. But surely those two uncertainties still amount to enough to trump marketing programmes that see your organisations disappear into the ocean of expensive but average promotions that make you look exactly like your competitors. Don't they?

---

[6] P. McIntyre, 'Marketing and media's troubled future: Mark Ritson, LinkedIn-backed global think tank and IPA UK's Fran Cassidy have a solution'. MI3, 10 February 2020. Available from www.mi-3.com.au/10-02-2020/business-has-stopped-believing-brand-marketing-next-time-think-long-and-hard-or-else [accessed 6 March 2021].

8 The risk of being fired

We're often pushed to accept marketing mediocrity over magic in the name of efficiency, predictability, speed and ease. We would be foolish not to worry that rocking the boat too much might lose us our jobs.

I didn't want the conversation around the concept of 'bravery' in this book to be theoretical. If being brave is to be a key factor in the success of B2B businesses, we need to understand it fully.

If bravery is only discussed in a glib, silver-tongued 'aspirational' manner, we run the chance of glossing over the jeopardy associated with being brave.

I asked all of my contributors to this book: 'What does being brave really mean to you?' Almost ever-present in their answers was the risk of losing their jobs.

In most of the conversations, risk existed as something of an undercurrent, an assumed and abiding threat. My chat with Doug Kessler, founding partner and creative director at Velocity Partners, however, brought the concern right to the fore.

> **Me:** *Is there an argument that the risk of losing your job shouldn't be seen as the reason not to do something you believe in or is that just naive?*
>
> **Doug Kessler:** *Maybe. It sounds kind of a privileged thing to say, but willingness to be fired, I think, is an important part of any job. I was told that early in my career. I started out at Ogilvy on Madison Avenue and was struggling with some bosses. I talked to someone I admired a lot and he said: 'Look, you gotta go in every day, willing to be fired. That's the only way to do any job well.' And I do believe it. I think if you would be fired for doing the right thing and pressing your professional view on what's going to work, you're good at what you do. This premise of course presumes from the start that you're talented, smart and committed; that you're not an idiot. So, if you're going to get fired for doing the*

right thing, yeah, you should get fired. You know, go somewhere else where you won't get fired for doing that.

Me: Are you comfortable having those words published in your name in my book?

Doug Kessler: Yeah. I am comfortable. I think, you know, you've got to know your life and where you are. You have to be prudent if you know that you're in a place that you're likely to get fired for doing the right thing. If you need the paycheque, well, don't go getting fired tomorrow. Line yourself up something better. And, you know, either quit or go for it – insist on doing the right thing by your company in good faith and see what happens. You might find you succeed. Being willing to get fired doesn't mean 'go out of your way to get fired'. It means you want the trust to behave as the expert in your field. You're showing you're willing to go elsewhere rather than do a bad job. And often that will work.'

Does your company deserve brave marketing?

It takes some bravery to aim for something extraordinary in a culture where it's easy to get mediocre stuff approved. You could have an easier life by settling for cranking out poor, underachieving and boring work, knowing you'll probably be alright. At least until commercial results demand a reduced headcount, at which point, as a marketer adding nothing anyone else can really quantify, you'll be vulnerable.

Conversely, if you're someone with a perpetual itch to do special work that makes a difference, there's a reasonable chance more complacent colleagues are going to find you quite an annoying presence.

In that way, your life at work will be harder but then, if the worst happens and your business does face the need to make redundancies, your unexpected or outlandish marketing success should serve to insulate and protect you somewhat.

'Some company cultures don't really accommodate those kind of people well and shouldn't have them,' states Kessler, 'They don't deserve them.'

Smarter employers, however, do listen when challenged by brilliant marketers with an appetite to do things better.

What does it look like to speak up?

One marketer I spoke to joined her firm as head of marketing. Despite her relative youth compared to the rest of her management team, it was clear during her interviews that she offered impressive strategic capability.

However, she was surprised to get the job as, during the interview process, she actually told the hirer she didn't really want it – she was there at the interview because a recruiter put her forward for it.

'Why don't you want the job?' her interviewer asked.

'Because the job spec and remit is framed around digital performance marketing and that's not me,' she replied. 'I'm a generalist strategic marketer rather than a digital specialist. I grow companies and use whatever tactics I need to do it.'

The hiring company loved that answer. She was immediately hired, invited on to the management team and told she could run marketing as she saw fit, including finding an additional hire to execute digital marketing. The marketer takes up the story of what happened next:

When I joined, I inherited a big report – our first really big piece of content. The CEO had commissioned a survey and serious budget had been spent.

But it wasn't good. The data was dodgy and there was no convincing story hook or angle.

I was worried about putting out – and being seen to own – a poor piece of work. We had little awareness at the time so maybe it wouldn't have been widely read, but still. It wasn't the strong, cornerstone piece of marketing content the company thought it was.

I actually thought: 'oh my goodness, I've made a big mistake because if this is what they think is a good piece of work, I've not picked the right job.'

It wasn't just my reputation I was worrying about; it was that of the company. My boss had told me the plan was to get the content written about in the media. I've done PR previously and knew the piece was nowhere near strong enough for journalists to take seriously.

I was worried because of who internally had already approved and bought into it. I knew I couldn't put my name to something like that but I didn't have a clear plan on how to handle it.

In the end, I arranged a meeting with my boss to discuss it. I was worried beforehand. I didn't know how he'd react. I'm the only woman on the management team and didn't want my first act in the job to lose credibility. I didn't think I was at risk of losing the job so early but I also didn't want to plant seeds of doubt in anyone, or come off as a troublemaker.

I expected my boss to say something to the effect of: 'I appreciate you taking the time to come and share your concern but this is what has been agreed, so just get on with it.'

Who wants to start a new job with that kind of conversation? Anyway, I proposed a new take on the content with a fresh strategy. I said: 'Look, no offence. I know a lot of money and time has been put into this — here's what I suggest and here are my reasons why.'

He replied: 'You're spot on and have just validated what I was thinking.'

What a relief. He trusted me enough to give me the job so he clearly liked me but my going to him with a strong opinion gained me extra trust. He now knows I'm someone who won't allow bad work; who will speak truth to power and face tough conversations head on. Doing what I did won me more licence to speak up in future when needed.

***

In 2010, a year into my editorship of Marketing Week magazine, I produced a new event for the publication called The Annual. It was to be a strategic day of learning for marketing directors and would feature a 'CMO-level-only' speaker line-up.

Promoted as Marketing Week's new 'flagship conference', it was a brilliant event that saw a sizeable audience hear experiences shared by the likes of Rick Bendel, then international CMO at Walmart, Anthony Thomson, the chairman of Metro Bank at the time, Daryl Fielding, then VP of marketing at Kraft Foods Europe, Babs Rangaiah, who was the global communications director for Unilever, and Brian Waring, who at the time was the vice president of marketing for Starbucks.

The Annual itself was a one-off. It was never repeated (surely placing it among the most haplessly named events in the history of marketing).

Despite its unfortunate absence of a legacy, the event content that day was fantastic. One of my favourite speakers that day was Syl Saller, global innovation director at Diageo. Her message was simple, clear and backed up with some extraordinary tales from her own experience. The directive Saller issued that day was to embrace, rather than avoid, uncomfortable conversations. The reason? Uncomfortable conversations, she had found, were largely the only types of conversations that result in any kind of progress or positive change.

Tough, uncomfortable conversations, like the one Doug Kessler describes above — the willingness to get fired for doing 'the right thing' — must, as he says, be weighed up against a number of factors, such as how insulated you are financially or whether there's another job waiting for you.

But we B2B marketers must start having these conversations more regularly — starting now — if we're to change our fortunes and take hold of our ability to realise our potential influence.

9 Unpicking three of B2B marketing's universal 'untruths'

One of the problems we face as B2B marketers is that we regularly get beaten up by a series of 'untruths' that everyone across the organisation has bought into and established as truth.

We know being brave is difficult and we know too that there are ways to make being brave a habit and build up the muscle over time.

One such act you can practise regularly is to speak the truth. If you unwaveringly speak a dispassionate truth with conviction; if you support it with empirical evidence, it's very hard for anyone to objectively call you out as wrong.

People may choose to disagree or argue but it's unlikely to result in your view being dismissed or leave you excluded from similar discussions going forward.

On the contrary, if you build yourself a reputation internally for providing a worthy perspective on crucial decisions, your colleagues will want to hear what you've got to say. Bosses don't make decisions alone – they require their best people to offer them a broad range of viewpoints.

When it comes to making strategic business decisions, there is rarely one single right answer and rarely does any one person have the best instinct or intuition every time. Instead, every forward move is a punt, where consensus is built around the most senior, the loudest or the best argument in the room.

If you're not regularly involved in those conversations, find a way in and practise becoming relied upon for customer, media or 'go-to-market' expertise.

A sidenote for younger B2B marketers

If you're in a junior position in B2B marketing, speaking uncomfortable truths to your managers is supremely difficult. It may be that you're not in a regular position of having the CEO's ear.

Regardless, you benefit from speaking the truth. The shiny halo accorded to someone both smart enough to be right more often than not and brave enough to speak up in an appropriate way is rare but sticky. Besides, if you're young and in B2B marketing, you have little to lose.

Ogilvy UK vice chairman Rory Sutherland has a rather bleak view of your perceived status. If he's right, you can turn your lowly position to your advantage by being a teller of tough truths:

> If you're a junior B2B marketer, you're a natural scapegoat. If things go wrong, it will absolutely be your fault. However, let's imagine you're a huge success. Well, then no one will credit marketing with that success. Engineers hate the idea that success could be attributed to marketing. Their status derives from how good they are as engineers.

> They see marketing as cheating. Why? Because how they view the world is that you're supposed to win on your superior objective characteristics. Marketing can never get the credit for doing anything original or unexpectedly brilliant; success can only be because of 'our brilliant product'. Your 'fancy' advertising was just a side-affair, a gimmick.

I hope this isn't the case but if Sutherland has accurately captured your day-to-day employee experience here, then what, really, do you have to lose by appearing to possess wisdom and character and developing the ability to speak uncomfortable truths from early in your career?

Speak 'the truth' about what?

Our discipline is rife with untruths – widely held beliefs that we need to have an industry-wide conversation about as an industry.

Untruth 1: ROI is above scrutiny as a worthy goal

Some of the biggest marketing brains out there believe we need to change the way we think about profit, and particularly the value we place on 'return on investment'.

The second metric, ROI, does not neatly equate to the first, profit. In marketing terms – prominently in digital marketing and B2B marketing – ROI doesn't always track and measure the right things. Often it measures silly, meaningless things and can both drive and reward bad behaviours.

I suspect more of us know this deep down than would be comfortable confessing it out loud in management meetings.

That's partly because shrewd B2B marketers with the intelligence and judgement to spend time and money investing in building their brands don't have an especially good proxy for ROI to offer.

And for their colleagues outside of marketing who are looking for any evidence that the marketing budget is being successfully managed, ROI is the most acceptable and easiest metric to understand.

The problem is that by allowing the conversation about our effectiveness to become focused on ROI, we've allowed ourselves to become the scapegoat.

Remember what Jann Schwarz said earlier: B2B businesses commonly use marketing efficiency as a proxy for marketing effectiveness but the two are not interchangeable.

We focus on efficiency because it's more straightforward to understand than the messy and serendipitous inputs that make for effective marketing. According to Sutherland:

> It's much easier to assemble a media matrix than it is to assemble a creative matrix.

> The amount of testing in media is excessive in relation to the amount of testing of creativity in the digital world. It works for you if you're the guy who's responsible for digital advertising. It's relatively easy to manipulate ways of being able to tell your boss at the end of each quarter: 'hey, last quarter we got so many leads or clicks but this quarter, with a slightly smaller budget, I've gotten us more.' And with that you've kept your job.

> The problem is it leads to a kind of incrementalism and an obsession not with what works, but what can probably be shown to work.

What this ignores, says Sutherland, is that your advertising and marketing often does the most work when it looks least effective. He gives the example of a sales rep selling solar panels:

> The most important thing you can do if you want people to buy your solar panels is to get the first person on the street to buy them. That's the difficult job and you pour all your energy and resource into it.

> But once you've got one, maybe two people on the street to buy your solar panels, getting interest from the third and fourth households is a much easier sell. From there, with the aid of social confirmation, sales on that street are likely to spiral.

In the example, you're working your hardest at the beginning, trying to close one deal. Your marketing will be running at full power but, with a single sale to show for it, on paper it looks an ineffective use of focus and resource.

By the end, you'll be fielding new interest galore while not having to toil particularly hard.

So, if you judge your advertising on its short-term effectiveness, you will think it is least effective when it's doing the most work and most effective when it's doing the least work, because most of the work is being done simply by what Robert Cialdini called 'social proof' in his 1984 book, *Influence*. A behavioural phenomenon where people copy the actions of others, believing that action to be 'correct' if enough people have already done the same, does not interpret well in a marketing strategy planning meeting.

Professor Mark Ritson, who has taught brand management to MBA students at some of the world's best schools while consulting for some of the most famous brands on the planet, calls ROI 'a dumb metric' which sends most companies the wrong way.

> If you take five years to properly manage the top of funnel brand-building strategy; really non-targeted stuff that has terrible ROI; if you put 50% of your budget there and keep the other 50% where it is in sales activation, you will make more money than you are now.

Marketing consultant, and one of two renowned authorities (along with research partner Les Binet) on marketing effectiveness, Peter Field describes a 'heartbreaking contrast' between what's best for ROI and what's best for long-term profit growth. 'The two are totally 180 degrees opposed.'

In 2019, *Marketing Week* magazine reported that Adidas admitted a 'short-termist' focus on efficiency rather than effectiveness had led to over-focusing on ROI and digital sales performance at the expense of brand building, a trend it was trying to reverse.[7] As Field observes:

> The Adidas story was classic. Why were they over-investing in digital? Because it gave them amazing ROI. Did it give them growth? Did it help them long term? No. I deal with plenty of B2B tech businesses who think the answer is digital but they forget to figure out the question.

> Eventually they realise that you've got to invest in brand.

---

[7] S. Vizard, 'Adidas: We over-invested in digital advertising'. *Marketing Week*, 17 October 2019. Available from www.marketingweek.com/adidas-marketing-effectiveness/ [accessed 6 March 2021].

Untruth 2: Gut instinct holds no value; data should remain the only factor in decision making

A couple of years ago, I hosted the key panel discussion at an event for a client at the Soho Hotel in London.

On the panel was Alexander Von Schirmeister, a former eBay CMO with senior stints also at Procter & Gamble and Telefonica and now executive Vice President for payments fintech SumUp.

He said something that day that helped plant the seed of the idea for this book: 'Gut needs to be part of the conversation alongside data, or too many decisions get left unmade.'

For a moment, Von Schirmeister turned to the rest of the panel – a line-up that included the CMO of British Airways and a couple of CEOs – and asked them straight out: 'What's happened to gut instinct? Where's it gone?'

All the panellists nodded their agreement. The problem with a conversation that champions the importance of gut instinct is that, by definition, there's nothing you can offer to back it up as an argument. No charts, no hard science. There's just personal and anecdotal experience. And on that panel, nobody was minded to disagree with Von Schirmeister.

It spoke to me and to several things I'd had going around in my head for a while. Let's consider gut instinct for a moment. We trust and rely on it to save our lives and keep us out of physical harm pretty much every day. Yet in a business setting, it's often seen as insufficient as a factor when deciding one's next move. Here was an experienced executive with a track record at some of the world's most famous companies admitting how difficult it is to inform colleagues that you trust your gut instincts when faced with 'the responsibility of 120 KPIs that hang over you every day'. When researching *Boring2Brave*, I called Von Schirmeister again to restart that conversation and this is what he said:

> I haven't changed my mind. We need to encourage our companies and executives – including CFOs – to allow for gut to be part of the conversation and the formula.
>
> Even though data's getting better and better, it's not perfect. And I haven't seen the tech, the formulas or models that allow for 100% accuracy in your decision making. It doesn't exist.
>
> If you wanted to rely on 100% accuracy in decision making, it means you'd have to leave 30% of decisions on the table because there's just no other justifiable way to go with them other than 'trust me, on this one... allow me to go with it'.
>
> And so the message for a CFO or CEO is 'sure, by all means optimise the 60, 70, 75 or 80% that you can measure. Make sure you're not being stupid with your

money. But know that the other 20% is me throwing a "Hail Mary". Let's take a punt because, who knows? You might win the lottery'.

To do what Von Schirmeister describes, it helps to have built up your goodwill in the bank and have the internal permission to get it wrong. If you can be part of building a culture that allows for a degree of experimentation, a culture more businesses boast about externally than actually promote internally, it would help.

What's certain is that most brands that win in the long term do so because they've built an emotional connection with the customer. That connection is not based on a formula or a mathematical media spend, nor is it because you happened to serve the right banner at the right time. It's based on someone's gut feel that resonated strongly – that other colleagues 'felt' was right even before the message or proposition underwent repeated tests.

Ann Handley, Wall Street Journal bestselling author and chief content officer at MarketingProfs, says that while she believes in the power of data to make decisions, she thinks B2B marketers are often guilty of 'over-indexing' on data:

> There are two other parts to decision making: there is listening – listening to our communities, our customers and our prospects – and then there is absolutely gut instinct in there. There are aspects of each one of those in every decision we make in B2B.

> When you under index on instinct and rely too much on data, that's where you get into a 'non-brave' space. Because if you need to prove everything, you won't take a risk and try something that hasn't been done before. And then we fail as marketers.

Von Schirmeister recalls the following:

> I was just having this conversation with the science people in my team. They're mathematicians who run the formulas and they're brilliant. I'm happy I'm not wasting my money. But 'also', I told them, 'screw the formula, we also need to do this'. They all asked why? So I told them: 'because I know it's the right thing to do'.

Creating a common language

The job of convincing others that data can comfortably be twinned with instinct will get harder as business functions necessitate the mixing of personality types.

The incoming general manager of the B2B unit at one of the world's big telecoms companies was nervous about his new role in the weeks leading up to the start date. He'd come through from a marketing background and part of his remit was to transform marketing content from the terrible state that the company recognised it was in. There had been no guidelines – hundreds of disparate departments and teams were making and distributing their own content without any kind of central owner or filter. 'How', he wondered, 'can I persuade my 300 marketers to adopt the same mindset when half of them are technologists learning to be marketers and the others are marketers learning to be technologists?'

Untruth 3: Anything we can't measure is meaningless

Fear can make us stupid. We make idiots of ourselves and our organisations by 'embracing stupid'. We let fear turn us from skilled operators into morons.

It's an easy situation to fall into and none of us are immune. I embraced stupid while working for a client some years ago.

The business was crammed with seriously talented people but they lacked marketing or communications experience.

Much of my work saw me launching and managing a digital marketing strategy to help them generate quality leads for the sales guys to follow up with.

I'd sit in the management meeting each week and give an overview of the latest result. The problem was that every time they saw a rise or a fall in the metrics – digital clicks, engagement with content, visitors to the website or someone filling in an online form – they would act. Each week a change in the numbers would have them setting us in a new direction, reversing something we'd already painstakingly decided, or just changing the strategy altogether. Full U-turns would occur in the space of a week.

Against my better advice, we'd look at the metrics several times a week. We'd act if there was a fall. We'd act if there was a spike. This wasn't data-driven insight. The brand was a newcomer to digital marketing and was still in the early throes of a test-and-learn phase.

They asked the team to track and measure everything, which meant we were actually measuring 'nothing'. We were tracking and reporting on miniscule changes in campaign engagement that should have been left well alone to play out over time.

Nothing I said over many months of working with them this way altered their insistence on seeing the data move in 'real time'.

The fastest way for us to decide to do something (if not exactly how to do it) was for someone to attend a meeting with a panicked look on their face, waving the latest promotion, ad or piece of collateral produced by a competitor. At that point there was a mad dash to instruct (instruct, not brief) the marketing team to produce something similar.

We were making too many decisions. Subsequently, we found ourselves repeatedly ripping up our own playbook and starting again.

Here's an exact conversation I had with my client.

Client: Hey Mark, how's it going?

Me: Hey, I'm good. How are you?

Client: Yeah, I'm fine thanks. So, I just wondered if you could shoot me a quick email with the latest marketing metrics we're seeing.

Me: Ok, I mean, I can do that. But I presented a full overview to you guys on Wednesday night. Today's Friday. I can take a dive in to HubSpot and pull some data out but I'm not sure you're going to see anything worth looking at in terms of change.

Client: Sure, I get that. But can you just give us a sense of any progress since Wednesday?

Me: There's a good reason why normally you'd probably look to report marketing metrics monthly or certainly no more frequently than once a week – especially when you've only recently launched a digital strategy and are in test-and-learn mode.

Client: Right. Why's that?

Me: Well, because checking the data too early or often increases the chance of us seeing what will be false positives or negatives. People do this all the time and it often leads to bad decision making because you're acting on trends that haven't had a chance to fully evolve (laughs)...

Client: (laughs) Sure, I get you. I totally understand.

Me: Cool.

Client: So, will you send some results over later today?

Me: Oh. Ok. Really? Can I ask though, what's behind the constant thirst to check the metrics? Is there something specific I can help with?

Client: Well, between you and me, I know it's a dumb thing to want to check the metrics three times a week or whatever, but that's how often I get asked for them. I'm having to have the conversation above me, which is why I need to have it with you.

Me: Got it. Would it help if you put me in that conversation with whoever it is, to explain why it's not best marketing practice to send this data up and down the company with such frequency? We've chosen a strategy; I think it's the right one. We should stick to it for the next 90 days or so – or even just a month – before we ask whether it's working.

Client: Probably best for me have the conversation so you guys don't have to. If you could just get me the data that would be good. Oh, and have a great weekend.

When I felt I could get away with it – if say, other priorities legitimately got in the way – I'd simply ignore the request. When pressed though, I'd give my client the micro metrics they wanted – the sort so meaningless and devoid of useful insight they should never be let out the door of the marketing department. Despite my best instinct, I'd give them what they'd asked for.

And that's how it works. That's how good companies *choose* to become stupid. Smart people ignore the specific expertise that got them hired in the first place and instead succumb to the fear of pushing too hard against what they know is bad practice.

How a clever company embraces stupidity

1   *A request comes down from the top of the hierarchy*

2   *The request gets passed on down the food chain by people who know it to be flawed*

3   *The request gets carried out by someone who should and does know better*

4   *Flawed data or information is sent back up to be reported and acted upon*

This whole process is carried out multiple times every day across our organisations by clever marketers deciding it's easier to just embrace stupidity than assert their expertise.

It would take a brave marketer to sit in a B2B organisation and assert that these 'universal truths' (and there are others) require scrutiny. But with blind belief in all three of these strongly held beliefs, we act to shrink the value created by our marketing efforts.

These untruths are so embedded that even as I'm writing this down to be published under my name, as a B2B marketer I feel pretty uncomfortable with questioning them. But we owe it to ourselves and our businesses to create the safe spaces in which we can explore these conversations, rather than shut them down.

10 Let's unbore ourselves

We spend a third of our lives working.

If you're unnecessarily doing something in a boring way that could be done in a fun way, you'd want to know about it, right?

It's a strange thing for anyone to voluntarily dismiss the opportunity to fire up the work they do each day with passion, creativity, honesty or humour. Yet that's often what many of us do in B2B marketing.

It sounds crazy, doesn't it? Especially when you consider that we're the 'customer department' of our organisations, the 'persuasion' department, the 'draw-people's-attention-and-make-them-like-you' department.

It stands to reason that charming, fun, sparkling marketing that is there to be enjoyed dramatically outperforms serious, technical marketing.

If you've read many technology analyst reports, you'll know they're typically heavyweight documents full of dense and dry copy. Few get close to anything one could describe as charming, fun or sparkling.

Zoe Scaman, founder of brand strategy consultancy Bodacious and former strategy director for ad agencies including Droga5 and Naked Communications, recently tweeted, bemoaning a bespoke report that one of the large consultancies had created for one of her clients. She called it 'shoddy' and 'awful', citing spelling errors, 'sentence structures that don't make sense', the kind of stock photography for which there is 'no excuse', 'laughably generic conclusions' and 'no real sense of direction'.

In one sense at least, Scaman could have been lucky. I've seen plenty of analyst reports and white papers with no photography or imagery at all. In fact, they've contained nothing by way of art direction to help readers break up pages and pages of solid, energy-sapping, tech-heavy and poorly laid-out copy.

Annabel Venner, former global brand director at Hiscox, comes into contact with countless white papers from B2B suppliers that she simply can't bring herself to read. 'If one of them just *tried* to tell a different story or even looked interesting and seemed to offer something unique,' she suggests, 'it would make a massive difference.'

We need to remember why we're in the job of telling stories and what we hope will happen when our future customers pick up and read our work. You'd love them to read it from back to front, right? You'd want them to adopt your selling messages or analysis as their own and share it with colleagues; for them to become your internal champion.

Now compare that customer outcome you aspire to with your own instinctive, physical response when you pick up someone else's overlong, dry, thought leadership white paper or get emailed another 'Why customer experience matters' blog.

Imagine now what it would take to plan and create something that would actually excite your customers and prospects, or make them feel smarter, or prompt them to stop what they're doing and pick up the phone to you.

Creating better, more original work every time doesn't have to signal the end of templates or scale. It just means templating and scaling the right things – like better storytelling and creativity.

Creativity, discussed more widely later in this book, often feels unwelcome to the more logical, operational or technical marketers among us. To many, creativity denotes a lack of weight or seriousness. Maybe some feel that employing a creative execution to convey their messaging risks coming off as smug and vacuous.

Done right, creativity doesn't mean any of those things; rather, it's simply the act of using imagination to come up with something original – and therefore fresh. It's stretching ourselves to come up with an idea or execution that target customers haven't seen before. Really, would any of us argue that's a bad idea?

You don't have to agree with 1950s New York ad agency man Bill Bernbach who believed creativity to be 'the last legal unfair advantage we can take over the competition'. But does anyone have an argument against designing marketing campaigns and activities that are distinct, interesting and maybe even fun for the target to read and share?

Would it help if we stopped referring to prospects as 'MQLs'?

One of the reasons we might fall into the habit of making dry, or as Scaman described in her tweet 'shoddy', output might be because we've inadvertently moved to completely dehumanise our customers in recent years.

I acknowledge it's probably useful to give a name to a group of prospects that are at a certain stage of readiness in the funnel to hear from each of our sales teams and that the term 'marketing qualified leads' looks to serve that function.

There are two elements to the term that make me feel uncomfortable, however. The first is that word *qualified*. Who says they're qualified? What makes them so? Did anyone ask the prospect? Like former Hiscox executive Annabel Venner, I've downloaded hundreds of white papers and reports with some vague intent to read them. Many have never been opened. Others haven't survived past my first glance at the front cover or contents page. Only the least discerning of optimists would watch me so quickly close the tab showing their content and take it as an indication that I'm so interested in what their brand has to offer that I'm more likely to be a future customer than I was only minutes prior.

But sure enough, because I downloaded their content once, they have my details and decide I'm in the market for receiving their regular communications.

As far as the marketer is concerned, I'm on his or her database and therefore on my way to being 'qualified'. As far as I'm concerned, I'm nothing of the sort.

The second thing that jars about the term 'marketing qualified lead' is that every time we abbreviate it to 'MQL' in daily conversations, it further culturally embeds the idea of our prospects as meaninglessly inanimate targets to 'hit', like racking up a score on a cheap space invaders game.

Jason Miller, head of brand at ActiveCampaign and content strategy expert, argues that we should stop making it our job to 'count MQLs and downloads' and start making it our job to 'change perceptions'.

When we refer to our prospects repeatedly as 'MQLs', we often forget that they're real people. Like you, they're having a busy and potentially stressful day, right now. If we're going to bother them with our message or promotion, they need it to be interesting. Or, at the very least, make sense.

As Jason Miller continues, 'Start with what's possible...':

There were marketers I worked with when I was at LinkedIn who told me they'd never heard of Scott Stratten or Seth Godin. So I asked them: 'Where do you get your inspiration from?' They'd say: 'I don't really know.' So I made it my job to find things to put in front of them to inspire them, to say: 'this is what's possible.' That's the biggest thing for any marketer: show them what's possible and then to compare, you show them what everyone else is doing: just pushing bad content out of the door. If you scroll through your LinkedIn feed right now, you'll see a bunch of mediocre stuff with a bunch of poorly written copy and you'll see people sharing it at record rates, especially those in the C-suite. And all it does is clog up the internet and our timelines with terrible content and poor execution: 'Check out our new blog' and so on. God forbid these people spend a little bit of time crafting something that actually draws some real insight and gives casual scrollers a reason to spend time on a great post or blog.

Case study: The Zendesk Alternative

In 2013, cloud-based customer service platform Zendesk, which provides ticketing self-service options and other customer support features, formed a fake struggling band called The Zendesk Alternative.

The marketing team was monitoring search terms and noticed a trend – people were using the term 'Zendesk alternative' to search for other platforms like Zendesk.

Deciding to win some organic search traffic off the back of the term, they created a fake music group. Zendesk bought the domain name 'Zendesk Alternative', created social media presence for the band on Facebook, Twitter and MySpace and listed the band's name on Bandcamp.

Parody videos of the band in rehearsals on YouTube, complaining between musical takes of customer service software buyers landing on their website, seemed so authentic it was almost hard to tell whether they were a spoof.

The impact and brand awareness generated propelled Zendesk to become market leader. The fake site, zendeskalternative.com, converted at a 95% higher rate than the main website. Zendesk attributed five closed deals in the first six months after launch to the campaign. It was fun. It was original. It grew the market and drove awareness. And it closed deals.

Imagine if we could make part of our living out of having fun, rather than merely churning out the dry stuff that bores us to write and that we've fooled ourselves into believing our prospects want to read.

11 Everyone has product info: You need a story

Everyone has information on their products. And at various points along the sales funnel, it's important to be able to share that content to answer the questions posed by potential buyers.

But having great technology within your business is not a differentiator. Everyone's got tech. The differentiators within your business are the talent you gather around that tech, how effectively you use it and what it enables customers to do.

So often in B2B marketing, however, the technical promises or specifications of our offering make up the opening header copy that first-time visitors see when they visit our websites and exhibition stalls or read our sales collateral.

In his book, *Hegarty on Advertising: Turning Intelligence into Magic*, BBH founder and creative director John Hegarty writes: 'The only space worth buying is the space between someone's ears. How you get your idea there is irrelevant. Technology is only a delivery system.'[8]

The technology that helps us all execute in our jobs as marketers is, without a doubt, awesomely powerful and developing all the time. But it's also accessible to everyone, cheap and pervasive. If everybody has access to the same technologies, then all we have to distinguish us as sellers of B2B technology is the quality of our thinking.

It's our marketing, brand and stories that have the potential to create standout and drive 'no-brainer advantage' for our customers.

---

[8] J. Hegarty, *Hegarty on Advertising: Turning Intelligence into Magic*. Thames & Hudson, 2011, p. 65.

I've served B2B technology companies across a number of sectors including ecommerce, retail, travel, finance and insurance, property, media and professional services. Broadly speaking, I don't see the same commitment to, or excitement about, out-thinking the opposition as there is about creating short-cuts through technology.

If you don't believe replacing bullet-point features and the technical specifications of your product with broader, more engaging stories would help generate sales conversations, try asking your customers and prospects.

Ask them questions – as detailed as your relationship will allow – on how they receive marketing from suppliers and how, indeed if, they read and absorb the contents.

Annabel Venner, former global brand director and partner at business and home insurance firm Hiscox, responds pointedly when asked how she engages with the marketing she receives from vendors.

> It would really help if suppliers worked harder to understand us before they send us stuff, or even demonstrate they can solve real problems. Otherwise, sadly, it comes down to this really functional kind of decision making based on feature tick-boxes.

I suggest to Venner that one of the problems vendors face is that they often compete with a cluster of others in a sub-market, all of whom perform roughly the same functions. Would it make a difference, I asked, if one of them told a distinctive, original story? Venner responds: 'It would make a massive difference. I receive so many white papers. I don't read any of them. I might occasionally download one to read later, but very rarely do I actually read it.'

Scott Brinker is VP platform ecosystem at HubSpot but also the editor of Chiefmartec.com, the renowned martech blog that produces the marketing technology landscape infographic, used by many as the benchmark for growth of the industry.

Brinker is a true technology enthusiast and advocate who believes we're living through the 'golden age of marketing'. Even he, though, has gripes about '75% of the market's shortcomings' in their ability to tell their story properly.

> There's maybe a top quartile that are really good at it, that offer a genuine narrative.

> But the rest of the market? I do that martech landscape infographic every year which involves visiting every one of the websites of those 8,000 companies. I can't tell you how many websites leave me thinking: 'You know, I do this for a living and I have no idea what you do'. Some them are absolute 'gobbledegook'.

Brinker admits that 'software is the easy part'. The really hard part for technology vendors to solve, he suggests, 'is the customer problem'.

> I'm not maligning the whole software development industry, but developing the software is not difficult. The bottleneck is understanding a genuine customer need and opportunity and being able to sell it. And not just sell it like, 'oh, I've hired a sales team, so I guess they'll sell it for me.' I mean, genuinely sell it, tell the story, have customers adopt and embrace it. Have it actually deliver on its promise, resulting in your advocate on the other side saying: 'yes, we adopted it and oh my goodness, it changed our lives.' That's the tough part.

Something about human psychology makes it easy for us to default to seeing so much in life as a straightforward choice of either 'A' or 'B'. Brinker though is urging a wider understanding that to be successful in anything, not just building a successful technology company, we need to start with a mindset that's comfortable twinning 'A' and 'B' and accepting both to be true. In this case, there's a need for both brilliant engineering and wonderfully arresting storytelling in order to succeed as a tech company. Neither discipline should be neglected. As Brinker continues:

> I'm an advocate for whatever tech makes possible. I do believe it's powering a golden age of marketing. In no way does that diminish everything else that marketing is or has ever been: from storytelling and empathy to a complete and intuitive understanding of who the customer is. Believe me, you have me 100% on this.

How do we shift from 'product spec sharers' to high-value storytellers?

In the previous chapter we met Jason Miller from ActiveCampaign. Miller was also the man behind 'The Sophisticated Marketer', one of LinkedIn's most successful ever content marketing campaigns. Miller thinks he has the answer for marketing teams looking to be less product-oriented and more story-led:

> When we bring on a new team member, the first thing I ask him or her is: 'Can you write?' That's the core skill of any good marketer. The rest is technology, which can be learnt. If you can't express yourself creatively, talk with feeling, articulate your passions or tell a story of some kind, you're going to suffer as a content marketer specifically, and probably as a marketer altogether.

The obvious problem with Miller's assertion is that it doesn't work for all of us and may potentially alienate some strong marketers with other skill-sets. Not all B2B marketers can express themselves 'creatively'. Far more members of our tribe are hard-wired to think about solving problems with logic as opposed to imagination or inventiveness, and don't feel comfortable with the notions of 'articulating their passions' or 'telling a story'.

That shouldn't stand in the way of creating better, more distinct marketing.

Margaret Molloy, CMO of brand strategy firm Siegel+Gale, frames the same challenge differently, preferring to think about it as 'simplicity' over 'complexity'. She observes the 'flawed belief' in many B2B marketers that loading up a company's messaging with information on features and function makes a product offering seem more premium. 'It's a myth,' states Molloy. 'Simplicity is the true form of elegance.'

She refers to a time when marketers thought using technical terminology would gain them respect and power. Maybe, she suggests, there was a belief they could command a greater salary by using 'advanced vocabulary'.

> Now, the power goes to the person who can simplify, who can synthesise all the inputs to create clear, fresh messaging; messaging that breaks through clutter with higher frequency and more emotional impact.

> Your target customers people are cognitively challenged at work. Simplify your message to cut through that and make it easier for your inside champion to advocate for you.

Want people to share your message? Tell them a good yarn

Margaret Molloy, global chief marketing officer, Siegel+Gale

Where branding intersects with demand generation, you'll find storytelling. The old model of B2B storytelling was the case study and there's still tremendous value in the case study. But storytelling matters too. There's a lot of research that says people's recall is better when you have a good story attached to it. The tendency in demand generation is to load up on facts, figures, features and function and completely neglect the storytelling, which is what demand gen marketers, I guess, consider the domain of branding. Great storytelling is simply something someone wants to pass along. Like a great yarn. That's the acid test. Is it a good story? Does it make people want to share it? The format is less important: whether it's a case study, a video or an Instagram live doesn't matter. The acid test of your story is will someone want to pass it along? It's the same test since ancient societies told stories back in the day. If someone shares, it's a good story. If it then drives you to act, it's also great marketing.

In any economic climate but particularly in downturns, businesses that over-rely on what they feel is superlative product, and neglect to think deeper to build a branded positioning – a 'mythology' – around their businesses, are often the ones wondering why they consistently battle competitors in a race to the bottom on price.

There's never a good time to define your positioning

If you haven't already established, articulated and traded on a distinct, powerful market positioning, there's never going to seem to be a good time to do it.

If you're a typical scale-up (though this applies to many more mature businesses too), your business is a few years old, you've a growing team across multiple markets and have a string of paying customers, but each week feels like a hamster wheel on amphetamines. Having worked in and around a number of similar businesses, I know what it's like to become addicted to the manic pace driven by needing the next closed deal to survive in an ongoing race against the clock.

But for all the 'winning' culture and every celebratory 'all-hands' meeting, there's often a silent, jarring undercurrent of recognition that something important is missing. Your software is potentially world-changing but you lack a story. That means nobody, including your employees, knows what you stand for. Without an immovable central belief system or promise, not even your best sales executive can articulate with enough potency why your product matters; why potential buyers should care.

Worse still, if you don't have a definitive positioning or identity – if you're merely the sum of your product features – your marketing and messaging will too easily interchange with that of your closest competitor.

When you lack distinct storytelling, brand positioning and messaging, you struggle for urgency in the 'sell'.

Boring2Brave task

If this feels like a problem you face as a B2B marketer, you need to stop the hamster wheel.

You or someone – maybe an external brand consultant – needs to lead your top people through a piece of work designed solely to figure out what distinguishes you in the market. To achieve sign-off for a decision to remove many of your most senior execs from their job of selling and growth for an entire day – maybe longer – is difficult. It feels unnatural and, to some, even unwelcome.

But brand positioning doesn't work unless everybody buys into it and knows how to use it. Unless there's been serious work done on making it real and bringing it to life across all your internal communications and processes along with every sales, marketing and customer service touchpoint, it'll be a waste of time. Take the responsibility for making sure the process – whoever facilitates and leads it – is sound.

If such an activity feels like a lot of work, that's because it is. But far from the 'navel-gazing' I once heard it described as by a sceptical chief operations officer, brand positioning isn't just the act of coming up with a catchy marketing line. High-value B2B storytelling comes with guidelines and rules on how to speak about your business and the benefits it drives.

Your product only has a short window before others catch up with or even leapfrog you. Your brand positioning and voice, however, is what will set you apart.

It's how you know McDonald's advertising from Burger King advertising without being able to see the logos. As my old agency Rebeltech used to say: 'B2B storytelling. You might call it marketing bullshit. We call it multi-million-dollar bullshit.'

Your Braver-lator pitch (sorry, not sorry)

How good is your elevator pitch, that 15–30 second 'spiel' we're all told to have ready for the moment when we find ourselves alone in an elevator with our target customer? If you want to understand whether your brand and business has a powerful positioning of its own, asking a number of your colleagues to recite their elevator pitches is a good start. Do you have one that you use and, if so, is it overly technical and product focused?

If the answer to that last question is yes, try pitching your line to your closest friend outside of marketing and technology. Make it someone you're close to. This is so you'll know if they're lying to your face about how 'interesting' they found it.

An elevator pitch is notoriously hard to nail but when you do get it right (you'll know from responses and the conversations that result), it's likely to be nothing to do with the tech.

Try drafting an elevator pitch around the answers to these simple questions:

1   What do you do?

2   Who do you do it for?

3   What makes you different from/better than the rest?

If your answers to those questions are anything less than razor sharp, crystal clear and of genuine interest to the next prospect with budget that you happen to meet, you've got some work to do. Yes, you can probably run a perfectly fine business without carving out yourself an appealing and distinct positioning and brand story but wow, you'll really be making it hard on yourself.

The bad news? Your instincts are right. Doing this job will require some time, some thought and is a potential distraction for some of your key people, on and off for maybe a month. Like I said earlier; there's never a good time.

The good news? Well, the potential list of good news is endless. You should feel well versed in the main points by now. But besides all that I've said in this chapter, one of the best things about you being able to tell a bigger, better story than merely explaining how your product works is that it's likely none of your competitors are yet doing it. You'd be the only player in your market with something different and interesting to say.

12 B2C: Bravery2Creativity

In previous chapters, we've explored the commercial opportunity of deploying creativity. Adopting creativity can have the effect of:

★ Driving up the numbers of prospects that read or embrace your marketing campaigns and messages.

★ Providing your product with confident and distinct standout from the rest of your marketing.

★ Ensuring your brand name and offer is memorable – strong recall influences purchase and long-term growth.

★ Relieving you of having to create boring work; bringing more opportunity to inject your work with imagination and invention and, while doing so, raising your profile.

Creativity and bravery are intrinsically linked. Creativity doesn't come without first making a decision to be brave.

Every problem has a creative solution as well as the more predictable and logical one. The London Underground station where I used to join the Tube network to commute each day was, for a long time, not a safe place to be after dark. Young people with nothing better to do would hang around and cause trouble. Anti-social behaviour was common, with incidents often spilling over into violence.

But one night something changed. The Tube station immediately became a less intimidating place.

Someone had come up with a bright idea.

Rather than paying for extra police officers to patrol at peak travel times, someone instead paid for a CD player and used it to pipe classical music through the station.

The station staff told me at the time that the move had an extraordinary effect, making the station environment 'calmer, softer and more pleasant'.

Bored kids stopped hanging around the station and moved on elsewhere. Anti-social behaviour disappeared. Commuters started walking through the concourse at a more relaxed pace and with their heads up, rather than rushing, shoulders hunched and avoiding eye contact.

One of the challenges of creativity is that it often relies on instinct rather than proof – the sort of ideas you wouldn't want to pitch at a boardroom full of people whose approach to solving problems is entirely dictated by numbers and logic.

Such creativity employed to solve problems almost always has its root in human understanding and behavioural insight (in this case, one assumes, the insight that it is physically impossible for a human being to mug another to the sound of *Ave Maria*).

Logical people don't like discussing notions such as creativity and bravery in business because they're difficult to visualise, let alone quantify. With creativity and bravery, 'you know it when you see it' but beyond that, they are hard to explain and encourage. This makes them especially hard to sell to sceptical colleagues as an opportunity to improve business performance.

Happily, Siegel+Gale CMO Margaret Molloy thinks she has an answer for that:

> In every category of B2B, there's more products that we need. You know you need creativity to help break through the clutter. The challenge though is that creativity is often defined too narrowly and it worries people.
>
> Creativity can be visual or it can be 'in the words', which I think feels scary and un-business-like to some. But it can also be in the strategy. When it's baked into your processes, it can be powerful.

Molloy notes that when creatives are being creative, separately from strategists being strategic, we miss an opportunity: 'Mix it together: when the strategists are creative because it's understood you need creativity to break through, and the creatives are being strategic in the service of business goals. That's when magic happens.'

Molloy is onto something with looking to articulate creativity in a way that feels useful, let alone anything that sounds more hyperbolic.

Tell the sceptics creativity just means 'simplifying stuff'

If you believe in creativity as a daily practice and approach but struggle to sell it to others, think about discussing creativity as it pertains to simplicity. Creativity is often less about adding frills on top of something and far more about stripping unnecessary layers away to achieve the same result with the most pared-down-as-possible approach.

The creative insight you need to create brilliant standout marketing is in your business already. When encouraging creativity, marketing effectiveness guru Peter Field tells B2B businesses that the key is to find the insight, linked to your brand or offer, that's going to unlock growth. That insight might come from a creative or it might come from a strategist. But it's about considering what you do as a business; what you offer your customers and then injecting that insight with an emotional story or experience to make it resonate.

Field recalls an advert from 2015 for Volkswagen commercial vans:

> For a pretty dry subject, it was built on some lovely, very human insights and observations about what it's like to be the proprietor of a small delivery business operating a fleet of vans. You know, you're like everybody's mum. The end line was VW at its best: 'Who looks after the person who looks after everything else?'

Molloy agrees that use of creativity in B2B has to be relevant; that businesses can't just rely on some unrelated and wacky idea. Creativity in a vacuum, that's dreamt up in isolation from the rest of the business, is of no value. Sceptics would be right to treat with suspicion ideas that have no discernible connection to the benefits delivered by your product or service.

And in fact, it's not just vital but also much easier to derive the creative insights you employ from the reality of what you do as a business – far simpler to do that than struggling for a creative idea with a blank page in front of you.

As Field observes: 'You need to beware the result coming off as cheap "e-wash" or emotional wash. Creativity isn't just a nice, warm, friendly thought. You have to start with what you offer as a business and ladder it up to some emotional benefit.'

The creativity challenge

One of the things B2B organisations would do well to start embracing is that, far from being vague, fluffy, or 'unbusiness-like', creativity can be a devastatingly powerful growth tool when exploited well.

The fact that it is not tangible, predictable or measurable makes adopting creativity hard for many stakeholders. In addition, the idea of building a culture of creativity doesn't perhaps sit well alongside the short-termism of a company's need to report growth with every quarter. But for those

CEOs and CMOs brave enough, driving a creative approach to both your internal operations and your marketing outputs leads to disproportionate opportunity and financial returns.

Three things that prevent B2B marketers from taking advantage of creativity

Creativity – The act of looking at a problem differently before solving it – can be transformative. Merlin Entertainments chief development officer Mark Fisher once told me the following three things are necessary ingredients of creativity. At the same time, they are also seen as barriers, and are therefore reasons why most businesses never exploit Bernbach's 'last unfair but legal advantage over competitors'.

Time – You never believe you have enough time to do anything differently or properly so you just keep on sprinting. That's a shame, because creativity requires you to physically make time to apply your imagination.

Outsider's perspective – If nobody in your business is practised in looking at everything as if they are using fresh eyes, you'll never see a better way of doing anything.

Bravery – Creativity requires courage. You're never going to get people to be creative if you don't let them try something new and, by definition, risky. The question to ask yourself is 'do you want to succeed more than you worry about looking daft?'

Case study: How thinking creatively took Toast from a company with a product to a category leader

Ann Handley, chief content officer at MarketingProfs

There's a company in Boston called Toast. It sells point of sale and management systems for restaurants. When Covid-19 hit and businesses were forced to close, one of the industries hit hardest was restaurants.

Rather than just sort of continuing as best as possible or taking a pause, Toast threw out the content calendar and asked themselves: 'what do our customers need from us?' Within a 72-hour sprint, they'd built a website called Rally for Restaurants. It wasn't Toast branded. It was about helping the customers. It appealed to consumers – a brave play for a B2B company – and gave them the ability to buy gift cards to their favourite restaurants to redeem in the future. Those gift cards functioned as a kind of micro-loan to bridge the gap for restaurants that had no revenue coming in. That was the first part. But then Rally for Restaurants evolved into a site helping restaurants to access all the government information and resources they needed to survive: 'What kind of funding do we have access to?'; 'What kind of government programmes can we *opt into?' Rally for Restaurants helped its customers navigate their way to survival. With gut instinct and a little courage, Toast managed to position itself as a leader, evangelising the entire category rather than its own business.*

***

To be fearful or suspicious of creativity – or to assume it has no place in the serious financial environment of a business – is to wilfully ignore the role creativity played in every great business or brand that ever existed.[9]

I wrote my last front cover feature for *Marketing Week* magazine in January 2012, just before I departed as editor to take a job in agencyland.[10] It was a feature on creativity and Ogilvy vice chairman Rory Sutherland was among those I interviewed. He was explaining why creativity is the perfect tool for brands to achieve their aims when there is little or no money available.

'Creativity is often seen as an extravagant luxury, self-indulgence. The reality is that the best creative thinkers spend most of their time asking questions like "does the project need this?" and "can it work without that?"'

Then he came out with a line I never forgot and have used countless times since; an elegant warning against the pervasive belief in the rational over the risky.

'If you think creativity is expensive, you should try logic.'

---

[9] Indeed, every great human achievement of any kind.

[10] M. Choueke, 'Swimming against the tide: Brands need to embrace a culture of creativity'. *Marketing Week*, 4 January 2012. Available from www.marketingweek.com/swimming-against-the-tide-brands-need-to-embrace-a-culture-of-creativity/ [accessed 6 March 2021].

13 The rebellion, language and science behind being brave

Being a fearless marketer doesn't mean being a stupid marketer. Bravery requires substance and, if nothing else, a sense of accountability to the goals your organisation is trying to achieve.

Restlessness is a necessary ingredient of bravery. Recklessness, not so much.

The most courageous marketers, doing the most impressive work (and by doing so, increasing the licence and permission for the rest of us to break out of our traditional B2B shackles), commit patience and effort to build the foundations of their story. They test it and either source or create the materials for it. They carefully build buy-in and belief from within their organisation.

That said, for B2B marketing to go from boring to brave, the industry needs rebels: people who have some kind of pathological need to bend or break the rules.

Somebody with the intent to rebel is present at the origin of every change. Rebels are often seen as disruptive, troublemakers who are best ignored. Actor and activist Martin Sheen once said: 'Every truth in history started as a blasphemy.' It necessarily took a rebel and a fearless moment to trigger each one of those transitions from blasphemy to truth.

So who are these B2B marketers among us that can make this difference? How do we identify them? And the question I hope you're asking at this point, are you one of them?

What you've read so far in the book was intended to build the case for and prompt a change from 'boring to brave'. In addition, I've sprinkled the pages so far with helpful *Boring2Brave* tips that will help you on your way.

The real shift in your marketing, however, is not going to come through isolated tactics and minor changes to your approach. Wholesale commitment to a braver and more powerful form of marketing can only come through a cultural endorsement across your organisation: where you are fully supported in what you're trying to do and why.

Shifting – or even as a valuable start, nudging and poking – that legacy culture to drive a change requires you to be a rebel.

If you're ready to rebel in the name of improving B2B marketing for all of us, what should you be armed with? What can you take with you to stand a better chance of turning what you might now see as 'boring' marketing into braver, more distinct and effective marketing?

The answer, familiar to anyone successful in business leadership, is to bring people with you. That means talking the language of non-marketers to convince them that the shift you want to make benefits the business.

This isn't just about building a great presentation to show in a leadership meeting or using brilliantly persuasive language. This is about understanding the language of culture change in business. Marketers, especially those of us in B2B, need to get much better at it.

If we're to spend the coming months persuading our businesses that there's a more effective way to go to market and grow market share, we need to use Culture Change Language.

In business, successful Culture Change Language needs to start with either one of the following two triggers:

1   Pounds, dollars or euros

2   Data

Remember, not everyone you need the support of is comfortable thinking creatively and talking about a change based simply on the merit of a great idea. Nor are they especially concerned with the customer metrics that marketing teams routinely track to follow their customer engagement.

The only way to change or open their minds and persuade them to consider a new way of doing pretty much *anything* is to couch that conversation in financial predictions or data-led evidence. Here's the data:

A study carried out in 2019 by guru marketing and advertising effectiveness researchers Les Binet and Peter Field for LinkedIn's B2B Institute provides some brilliant pointers for all of us.

After years of sifting case studies and publishing hard evidence on effectiveness in B2C marketing, the 2019 report commissioned by LinkedIn's B2B Institute was the first time our B2B world came under Binet's and Field's focus.

The report, 5 *Principles of Growth in B2B Marketing*, found that some of the key rules for effectiveness in B2C marketing also apply to B2B.[11] It concluded that five practices in particular – routine to B2C marketers – are also common to the most effective B2B marketing case studies while hardly being utilised by most B2B marketers.

In fact, a survey of marketers by LinkedIn Marketing Solutions suggested many B2B marketers are doing the exact opposite of following these rules – for instance, concentrating wholly on sales activation rather than balancing the focus across activation and brand marketing; and placing more belief in loyalty-based strategies than customer acquisition.

Binet and Field's five findings for effective B2B marketing[12]

• **Invest in share of voice**

There is a strong relationship between market share growth and investment in advertising measured as 'share of voice'. The relationship is very similar to that observed in B2C, implying that advertising works just as hard in B2B as B2C.

• **Balance brand and activation**

Advertising investment should be balanced between long-term brand building and short-term sales activation (such as lead generation). Investment in both is needed, but B2B appears to require more activation than B2C, with an optimum of around 45% brand, 55% activation.

• **Expand your customer base**

Broadly, there are two ways a brand might grow – either by gaining more customers (increasing penetration), or by selling more to existing customers (increasing loyalty). Some, working on received wisdom, believe that loyalty is likely to be the more profitable route, because acquiring new customers is expensive. In B2C, the overwhelming weight of empirical evidence tells us otherwise. Decades of research by the Ehrenberg-Bass Institute shows the main way brands grow is always by acquiring new customers. As they do so, they always get a bit more business from existing customers as well as broad reach advertising campaigns reassuring existing customers that they've made a wise, popular and safe choice. Loyalty is never the main engine of growth and only ever increases when penetration does. Even with our limited sample

---

[11] The B2B Institute, 5 *Principles of Growth in B2B Marketing: Empirical Observations on B2B Effectiveness.* LinkedIn, 2019. Available from https://business.linkedin. com/marketing-solutions/b2b-institute/marketing-as-growth [accessed 6 March 2021].

[12] The B2B Institute, 5 *Principles of Growth in B2B Marketing.*

of B2B cases, customer acquisition strategies tend to be much more effective than loyalty strategies, and reach strategies (which talk to customers and noncustomers together) tend to be the most effective of all.

- **Maximise mental availability**

Campaigns that build 'mental availability' more strongly tend to be more effective. Mental availability is the extent to which the brand comes readily to mind in buying situations, triggered by a combination of high saliency and strong associations with the category.

- **Use emotion**

Emotional campaigns (ones that try to make prospects feel more positively about the brand) are more effective in the long term than rational campaigns (ones that try to communicate information). According to the IPA Databank, B2B campaigns built out of strategies that rely on emotion are up to seven times more effective than those that are not. The kinds of emotional approach required will be very different in B2B from B2C, but the principle applies across both. This is because emotional campaigns are better at brand building. However, rational campaigns are better at short-term sales activation, so a balanced campaign will incorporate both.

B2B and B2C marketing: More similar than we thought?

Were Binet and Field surprised by how closely their findings aligned with effectiveness in B2C? Binet shared his thoughts with me:

> Well, there was comparatively limited data sample in terms of the number of pieces of work we looked at, but yes, we were surprised.
>
> One of the most surprising findings was the one about share of voice. In B2C there's always been a robust relationship between share of voice and market share growth. We could see in the B2B data exactly the same relationship and it was highly statistically significant.
>
> Several other things came out that we feel B2B marketers looking for an advantage can grasp and use: the emotional versus rational, the penetration versus loyalty and so on. It was surprising that some of the really major relationships in marketing seem to be identical across B2B and B2C.

Binet and Field didn't have a great deal of time to fully gauge the response of B2B marketers before the world of events shut down to protect against the spread of Covid-19.

They did speak to some live audiences though and felt their work was met with a warm, if somewhat mixed, reaction. As Binet comments:

The stuff about share of voice isn't something people talk about in B2B or a metric that they widely use.

And I suspect the bit about focusing on market penetration versus a drive for greater loyalty was contrary to how B2B marketers think strategically. It's an article of faith for many in B2B that growth comes through getting more business from existing customers. So while I saw some people nodding along, I suspect many were wondering why they were being told everything they've been doing is wrong.

Who knows? I imagine some of the people actually working in B2B who saw our work felt like: 'who are these two tossers coming in and laying down the law on how B2B marketing works when they've clearly never produced a B2B campaign in their life?'

Binet's words held some prescience. Soon after I spoke to him, I interviewed one of the most knowledgeable and connected people anywhere in B2B. Joel Harrison is editor-in-chief and co-founder of B2B Marketing – a company providing content, events, training, reports and a magazine to more than 75,000 subscription members.

I was a trade magazine editor and there are more than a dozen others I know pretty well. In terms of the effort Harrison makes to listen and add value to his community, he is one of the best out there.

Harrison smiles wryly when I bring up the Binet and Field report and their findings.

I'm smiling because people who are as reputable as those two, who spend all that time writing about marketing, suddenly decide to wake up one day and decide to write about B2B.

Every time someone like Marketing Week talks about B2B, I'm like: 'Oh, really? Fifteen years later, you've finally worked out that B2B exists? Are you really interested?' I understand it's an emotional reaction but I do get a bit cross about it.

To a certain extent, I tell Harrison, he is right. When I was editor of *Marketing Week* between 2009 and 2012, we did a pretty poor job of covering B2B marketing. It's the one regret I have about my time in charge of the publication. Harrison continues:

The honest answer is that their findings never really surfaced to me. I did see Peter Field talk at an event, which was really good. He did a great job trying to take B2B leadership to a different level. Someone has to do it and they've done well. Hats off to them.

Referring to the research though, Harrison says it annoys him when B2B marketers are described as lacking understanding of brand:

The reality is they don't have it in their remit to own the brand. They don't have the trust of the board. It's not a bearing on the quality of the marketers. It's simply that B2B organisations more often see brand as the personal fiefdom of the CEO.

Running a B2B brand campaign: How to beat the system

Joel Harrison, editor-in chief and co-founder of B2B Marketing

Honestly, I think most B2B marketers just accept that they don't 'own' brand building; that's the way it is. Marketers can do demand generation activity that builds the brand in the background. But there are also ways of beating the system. One of our members is a VP of marketing from a global technology services consulting firm. When she started in her role, she had a brand campaign created by her agency, sat there ready to go. She went to the board for approval and they said: 'Why are you doing this? What's the brand got to do with you?' They told her to freeze the campaign, stop everything. They just weren't comfortable with marketing talking about brand. So about three months later, she made subtle changes to the messaging in the campaign and called it a lead gen activation. Everyone loved it. It was the same campaign. Only, this one actually got out of the door and was very successful. Marketers are anxious to do more but until that happens, they're getting on with doing the things they are given the latitude and trust to do.

Harrison's story about his member is great. But I still find the first line jarring: 'B2B marketers accept they don't own brand building.' I don't accept it.[13]

Binet and Field's research may be the first academic exploration of what makes for effective B2B marketing. Their findings may be based on relatively limited data compared to their B2C work, but we'd be sleeping on the job if we didn't at least explore how embracing those five recommendations might increase our lot:

1   A contribution to stronger, more sustainable growth for our businesses.

---

[13] In this regard, things are changing in real time. Harrison emailed me in March 2021, shortly before this book went to print, to report that the Covid-19 pandemic had affected how B2B marketing views 'brand' and who owns it. 'Attitude to brand has changed a lot during the pandemic,' he wrote. 'We spoke about this last summer. That's a long time ago in the current atmosphere. Brand comes up really highly [in surveys] from B2B firms. There's generally been a reassessment given the radical change in circumstances.'

2   A greater respect for and understanding of the value and influence marketing can contribute.

3   Increased profile and better, more fulfilling careers.

14 The thing about B2B nobody ever cared to acknowledge

If asked to boil down all the findings from Binet and Field's report, *The 5 Principles of Growth in B2B Marketing* – looked at in the previous chapter – into one overall learning, it would be this surprising conclusion:

What makes B2B marketing effective is more similar to that which drives B2C marketing effectiveness than it is different.

Here's a hypothesis worth exploring: B2B and B2C marketing aren't that different when it comes down to their empirical formulas. Much of the long-assumed distinction between them is the result of artificial layers of expectation and human bias placed there by us, the practitioners.

If this supposition turned out to be right, it would give B2B marketers a whole new set of guidelines and possibilities to test and investigate in the service of growing their company's market share. 'I don't believe in pure play B2B teams or agencies,' states Margaret Molloy, whose global branding company Siegel+Gale works with some of the world's biggest brands in B2B *and* B2C:

> Neither our users nor our buyers live in a vacuum. Distinctions like B2B and B2C don't really hold much value. Ideas cross-pollinate between industries and categories. If B2B brands decide to go online, for example, they base the experience they offer and the expectations they promise on their own experience with brands like Amazon and Google.

The trick to providing comfort for clients and colleagues who cling to traditional boundaries and differences between the disciplines, argues Molloy, is often cosmetic. 'Don't get too hung up on the vocabulary,' she says. 'Instead get hung up on the outcomes.'

> When I'm working with law firms and professional services companies, the word 'brand' feels fluffy and is seen as a waste of money. So instead I talk about reputation. Let's 'build our reputation'. That's suddenly very appealing to these kinds of clients.

Annabel Venner also has deep experience as a senior marketing leader in both B2B and B2C. Former roles include more than a decade as global brand director and partner at Hiscox, an insurer with both B2B and B2C customers. That position followed a nine-year stint as a senior marketer for Coca-Cola.

'I didn't see our marketing at Hiscox as B2B or B2C,' explains Venner. 'The absolute principles are exactly the same.'

> In fact, I genuinely felt much closer to our customers in the B2B setting than I did at the consumer packaged goods companies I've worked for.

> At Coke, you're basically there to make a good advert every year. In B2B you have so many more points of interaction where you really make a difference to people's lives.

> You have to work harder because the conversation that customers are looking for when they call your contact centre or buy from you online is really important.

> You're not passing off that interaction to a grocery retailer like you effectively do when you work at packaged goods companies. At Hiscox, you properly 'own' the customer. I had much more responsibility as a marketer at Hiscox than I did at Coca-Cola.

The global value of B2B marketing is rising: Why doesn't our confidence reflect that growth?

As a B2B marketer, you're part of an enormous global industry. The value of B2B marketing, though hard to define or measure, is significant.

According to Statista, B2B digital ad spend in the US was more than $6bn in 2020 and B2B trade show market value in the US was $15.5bn.[14] Globally, trade shows are expected to surpass US$40bn by 2023 and that represents 'slow' growth compared to digital marketing spend.

But our experience of B2B marketing on the ground doesn't often reflect that sense of a highly valued industry experiencing dynamic global growth. More commonly, it feels like being on a mindless treadmill

---

[14] A. Guttmann, 'B2B marketing – statistics & facts'. Statista, 6 October 2020. Available from www.statista.com/topics/2495/b2b-marketing/ [accessed 6 March 2021].

— chasing any lead regardless of its worth in what feels like no more than a subservient sales support role.

The frustrated among us know how much time, energy and opportunity we waste keeping the cogs spinning in a process measured in metrics we know are meaningless.

It's getting worse: the sheer pace of growth in the number of B2B tech vendors and platforms every year means it's ever harder for our complex, technical, product-focused sales messages to rise above the noise of the market.

Our industry might be in growth but by accepting such an ineffectual, sterile and hapless role, we inadvertently sell our organisations short while serving to stunt our own career potential.

Anything that can aid the mission of encouraging B2B marketing the world over to quit its 'submission and safety' posture and get brave is worth consideration and study.

The Binet and Field report legitimately opens the door for us to scrutinise what can be borrowed from the best of B2C marketing. But what does that look like? What should we be doing?

I asked Annabel Venner how she dealt with the jump from consumer marketing to marketing to businesses:

> I was lucky when I joined Hiscox. My boss at that time was ex-Procter & Gamble [consumer packaged goods manufacturer]. His boss was ex-Coca-Cola and ex-Diageo.
>
> By the time I joined, the business had already had all the really difficult conversations; had proven the benefits of marketing and strongly believed in the power of emotion.

In addition, Venner says, when she joined, Hiscox had recently appointed London-based creative agency VCCP. The agency's idea for the business was built around demonstrating it understood its consumer with the use of emotional creative, supported by functional messaging. 'So it wasn't a battle I had to fight,' explains Venner. 'The door was already open.'

Does B2B need an influx of B2C marketers to drive change?

Does B2B marketing need more B2C marketers to come in and influence B2B marketing by demonstrating what's possible? Could it really be that simple (and irritating) an answer? As Venner comments:

> If you can persuade more B2C marketers to jump, it might help. Some of them won't move — there's still an unfounded stigma about B2B being inferior to B2C.

> I have a different opinion on that but if you can persuade them to come, they can help fight the battle.

> Or you need to have senior marketers in the B2B environment who are up for a fight and banging the drum within their own organisation to try doing things differently.

Nicole Lyons, head of marketing at industrial sector marketplace Axora, believes bravery is less about someone's career background and more about who a person decides to be:

> I always followed my heart over my head if something didn't feel right. When something needs changing up, I'm not afraid to make a decision. There's a feeling of 'what's the worst that can happen?'

> I know not everybody is the same. There are plenty of people who are happy to play it safe and don't care about being brave. But I also think there are a ton of brave people out there in B2B marketing who don't know how to apply it. They don't know how to make a difference. I think they feel trapped.

It would be far easier to ignore any urges for increased influence in shaping strategy or more scope to do the marketing job the way you think it ought to be done. Contentsquare marketing director Matthew Robinson observes: 'The easy thing to do is always pull back and deliver really safe marketing campaigns. No one in B2B will complain about you staying right in the middle of the road.'

But the opportunity for us and our businesses is way too great for that. As alien or counterintuitive as it may feel to some, we have the chance (maybe even the responsibility) to mine unfamiliar sectors, industries and yes, B2C, to find new approaches with a track record of success.

Not all B2B marketers will accept this. Some will find reasons not to, which as ever will leave the landscape wide open for those who do want to see if they can learn something new, to gain competitive edge. According to Margaret Molloy:

> Not every company has the mindset to go looking outside their category to find inspiration in another category.

> Some B2B companies don't connect those dots. When we go to pitch, they'll say: 'We only want to see examples of your work in our category.' I don't love that. It's an indicator of a closed mindset. It sets up straight away a limit on their view of brand or what great marketing can do.

That B2B marketing has far more in common with B2C marketing than we first thought will come as heresy to some – especially anyone who feels they stand to profit from B2B marketing staying as it's always been.

While there are, and will always be, some key structural distinctions between B2B and B2C marketing – such as the shape of the customer journey – content wise I'd argue on the side of Binet and Field's findings. There's room for emotional and even humorous creative; there's reason to reach beyond the bubble of your current customers and database and so on. It's a view that seems to be getting increasing exposure. In September 2020, *The Drum* magazine's US editor Kenneth Hein wrote a piece asserting that the Covid-19 pandemic had accelerated a trend for B2B advertising starting to resemble B2C advertising more and more.[15]

One example Hein cites was one of my favourite campaigns in 2020. To promote its Signals virtual conference in the autumn, digital customer engagement platform Cheetah Digital created a series of very funny ads for YouTube starring Mötley Crüe drummer Tommy Lee and his wife Brittany Furlan-Lee.

If Cheetah Digital was trying to step away from industry-standard, slick and shiny event advertising to tell its market about Signals 2020, it had enough obvious assets it could have used. Seth Godin and Jay Baer were among the genuine B2B marketing rock stars that Cheetah Digital could have called on to help drive interest and bookings.

What makes the Lee and Furlan-Lee ads so memorable is not only the random juxtaposition of bona fide rock and roll celebrities discussing their excitement at sessions on personalisation and omni-channel loyalty, but also that they put in such good performances.

If you want to check them out, maybe start with my favourite in which Furlan-Lee has to let the Biden election campaign down because a planned meeting with Biden's team clashes with a talk at Signals about data-driven engagement by Michael Stutts of Bloomin' Brands.[16] The bit that kills me is Furlan's wholehearted impression of Kenny G who she suggests as a replacement.

There is already a trickle of superlative marketing campaigns coming out of B2B companies – ideas and executions that would not look out of place in the B2C canon. That trickle will become a flood in the years to come as B2B marketing grows in confidence. You can try to hold out and continue marketing the way you've always known it, or grasp the nettle and be one of the first to show the way forward.

———————

[15] K. Hein, 'That was a B2B ad? How the pandemic forced business marketers to pivot forever'. *The Drum*, 22 September 2020. Available from www.thedrum.com/news/2020/09/22/was-b2b-ad-how-the-pandemic-forced-business-marketers-pivot-forever [accessed 6 March 2021].

[16] Cheetah Digital, 'Brittany Furlan-Lee & Tommy Lee can't miss Michael Stutts of Bloomin' Brands at Signals 2020'. YouTube video, 24 September 2020. Available from www.youtube.com/watch?v=XjATHtIfBoo [accessed 6 March 2021].

15 This is the winter of our dissed content

Nobody needs that next piece of content you're about to produce.

No one's waiting desperately for it.

There's a Content Mountain because, as B2B marketers, we constantly overproduce. And when there's a surplus of something it drops in value.

A corporate communications specialist at one of the world's top five banks was bemoaning 'the state of our content marketing':

We make way too much content.

The more content we produce, the more I fear it gets ignored. We're measured on how much content we produce rather than how well it's received or what it achieves for us.

Trust me, when you've seen any single one of our social media quote cards, you've pretty much seen them all. Our whole content process, from the calendar to the execution, is a mess.

Content calendars can be useful but they can also be the reason so many B2B marketing teams run into trouble. Once a content calendar has been created and signed off, it often becomes a brainless 'de facto' boss to the content marketing team; robotically demanding specific content formats on specific days. I've seen marketers opt out of any cognitive judgement or decision making in terms of story, message or even quality once they have a time-sensitive tick box in the form of a content calendar.

Boring2Brave actions

Here are four tips to consider when looking to create smarter, better content.

1. Don't settle for the obvious take

On the first day of my postgraduate diploma in print journalism, I heard something I've held on to throughout my career as a journalist and creator of marketing content. It's an incredibly simple lesson that few B2B marketers act upon.

'How to write a good opinion piece,' I was told, 'is to take something that absolutely everyone universally agrees with, and find a smart way to disagree with it.'

We provide massive value to our readers by ensuring originality – coming up with an angle nobody else has – as well as controversy: being someone with the opposite view to everyone else.

This doesn't mean you should pretend to be someone you're not, or fake a controversial point of view you don't believe in, just for the sake of being different.

What it does mean is that when something newsworthy happens in your industry or sector that you think requires you to write a blog for LinkedIn or Medium, stop for a moment before you write anything and take time to sit and think.

American journalist and literary critic Burton Rascoe said: 'A writer is working when he's staring out the window.'

Imagine the 30 or 40 blogs about the same news event that you're likely to see published and distributed across your social media timelines in the next few hours. Most of them are going to say pretty much the same things. How can you make yours refreshingly different and memorable?

Or, if you're going to log the same analysis and conclusions as every other 'thought leader' out there, is it really worth you taking the time? Is anybody going to read or share it?

Maybe, maybe not. What they absolutely will share is the one blog post or article about said news event that features a different angle or offers an alternative perspective.

That stands a greater chance of being the piece of content your community shares with the recommendation: 'if you only read one piece about XXX today, make it this one!'

But how do you write that blog post, the one everybody shares?

2. Become a journalist

Here's how I may have thought about writing the blog during my journalism years.

★ What will everyone else say about this… and therefore what else can I say that's fresh?

★ Do I know anything about this event that nobody else knows? Is it possible I can add context, background information or a parallel story? Can I move the current story forward?

★ Do I know anyone involved or related to the event that I could call quickly and get some expert or even insider perspective, on or off the record?

★ Can I paint or frame this news event in a different light? Can it be explained by a seemingly unrelated wider trend?

★ Do I have to write this today? Is there value in letting everyone else crowd the field for the next 24 hours or even the next week, and waiting for the story to play out further?

3. Slow down; craft takes time

I used to have an incredible boss. There was so much to admire about him. However, one of the difficult jobs I often had while working for him was to slow him down.

As well as being brilliant at his job, he was an elite athlete. This meant his body and his mind worked much faster than most people's. He could never stop thinking or wanting another challenge or problem to solve. As a result, he'd have maybe four or five 'big ideas' a month for new campaigns he'd want out in the market.

This wasn't practical, useful or even enjoyable for his colleagues who felt they had a choice of either ignoring many of his requests, or swirling around in his constant chaos and maelstrom of 'disposable' campaigns.

When I first joined the team, he sometimes gathered people for a 'blogging session'. The aim was to build up a pipeline of content for the coming few weeks. A session would typically last about an hour. Every person attending was on the hook for producing a blog. Hardly any of them were specialist writers. They were loyal and dedicated though, so they produced blogs. And these blogs would be put into the content calendar.

I'm a writer. If I'm going to produce a blog, it's going to take me a lot more than an hour. I want to read enough news, amble aimlessly around the internet and read around a specific subject, just to figure out what my topic is going to be and exactly what I want to say.

The likelihood of anything I produce from a standing start in the space of an hour being good enough to publish in the name of your brand is miniscule.

We need to stop thinking about content in units of 'deliverables' and start seeing content in terms of its quality and potential for bringing your community together behind a powerful idea.

4. Take design seriously

'Everything is designed. Few things are designed well,' said Brian Reed, front-end developer and musician.

Everybody is creative. Strangely though, some people like to pretend – even boast – that they're not. I once knew a chief operating officer that would make and present decks with the most hideous slides I've ever seen.

There would be floating pieces of bad clip art, random luminous-coloured shapes and arrows, diagrams with no grounding or border. Nothing would be lined up on any of the slides so it was hard to make sense of where your eye was supposed to start or finish.

When I watched him present at meetings, he'd often open with the line: 'I make no apology for the state of my slides; I have the creative and design sense of a newt...'

He would smile when he delivered the line and people in the room would laugh.

But what he was actually saying was that he couldn't be bothered to put any effort into making his awful slides legible or in any way easy to look at. So they weren't just awful; they were also falling short of their purpose.

People who proudly (why?) see themselves as uncreative will often tell you at the beginning of a project – a presentation deck or a piece of marketing collateral perhaps – that they don't care about design.

It's happened to me several times in my career. Maybe it's happened to you. Someone will approach you and ask for your help to create something with an impossibly short lead time.

You set out a plan around their needs and naturally that plan, however rushed, will include building in design time.

They tell you imperiously that they 'don't care how pretty it looks, as long as the "content" is right'.

And your heart sinks. Because it's a lie.

Everyone cares about design. The problem is that some people think they don't until you near the project deadline with your 'best but inevitably wrong' guess at how they want it to look, at which point the whole conversation becomes about design.

As communicators, it's our responsibility to challenge colleagues – or just about anybody – who, for whatever reason, don't think they care about design.

Turn it into a financial decision for them, because they'll care about that. Quote Trello creator and web programmer Joel Spolsky to them. Spolsky said: 'Design adds value faster than it adds costs.' And then beg them to engage a designer and issue some sort of design brief.

The write stuff

Jason Miller is head of brand at ActiveCampaign and a former group marketing manager, global demand generation, social media and content marketing at LinkedIn. Miller told us in an earlier chapter that the first thing he asks for in a marketer is that they write well.

How do you know if you're a good writer though? Everyone thinks they can write – right?

The thing I always hope qualifies me as a writer is that I've been writing for a living since I started getting paid to do stuff. But unless you're a Pulitzer Prize winner or a *Sunday Times* bestseller, nobody gives you a certificate for being a great writer.

More importantly perhaps than how sure you are as a writer is this: whether you think you're any good or not, can you improve?

Now we're talking. If ever there was a right question.

Ann Handley might be one of the most famous figures in B2B content marketing. Chief content officer of MarketingProfs, co-founder of ClickZ and keynote speaker, Handley is also bestselling author of *Everybody Writes: Your Go-To Guide to Creating Ridiculously Good Content*.

I asked Handley what good writing looks like and what B2B content marketers need to know, if indeed, they don't already:

> When I talk about good writing, I'm not talking about literary-quality writing, although if you are capable of that, good for you.
>
> To me, the essence of good writing is the ability to state your case with brevity and clarity, with respect for the person you want to be read by. Communicate in a way that will resonate with him or her.

It's notable that Handley's advice is to focus on an individual person rather than trying to connect with a faceless business audience. She continues: 'Yes, think about the individual you are trying to connect with. Not an audience, but an individual intimately; that's the heart and the mind of the person you are trying to reach, especially in B2B.'

Case study: The Sophisticated Marketer's Guide – secrets of 'content greatness'

When Jason Miller was at LinkedIn between 2013 and 2018, he dreamt up and executed one of the greatest content marketing campaigns of all time. Certainly, *The Sophisticated Marketer's Guide* was the most successful content campaign LinkedIn has ever run, achieving 18K% ROI and becoming an owned media empire, including category verticals, niche spin-offs and a marketing podcast, which debuted at number 3 on iTunes' marketing podcast chart and continued for eight seasons garnering more than 200,000 downloads across 110 countries.

Here, Miller shares some of the lessons behind the success of *The Sophisticated Marketer's Guide* campaign.

'Write it like an author writes a book'

When I came up with The Sophisticated Marketer's Guide, it was completely ripping off the idea of the 'big rock' pieces of content I'd been involved with creating at Marketo. I'd worked with Maria Pergolino and we'd created The Definitive Guide to Marketing Automation, The Definitive Guide to E-mail Marketing, the definitive guide to whatever the hell conversation we wanted to own. This was their idea, not mine. The concept wasn't ever to write some easy, quick, sh**ty e-book, right? It was to create 'big rock' content that could feed your story needs for a whole year. It's got to be good. If you're going to write a book, write the book like you're an author. Publish it and then revise it every single year. Like David Meerman Scott does with The New Rules of Marketing & PR. So when I came over to LinkedIn, I stole that same concept and intent. 'What's the number-one question right now that we can answer better than anyone else?' It was, 'how do I market effectively on LinkedIn?' That's where 'Sophisticated Marketer' was born.

'No source of inspiration is illegitimate'

I've always had a passion for music. A lot of my ideas are inspired by the artwork on album covers. Why not? These album covers were, after all, tested, proven pieces of artwork designed to get attention. Around the time we started developing The Sophisticated Marketer's Guide, I was carrying this CD around called Sophisticated Jazz Sounds. The original Sophisticated Marketer creative was based on this CD cover. It was vector art with a cigarette in an ashtray and a Martini. One that got us in a lot of trouble is a book we did called How to Create Your First Big Rock – a question we were getting regularly from sales. I had this vision for the cover. It reminded me of the cover of AC/DC's The Razor's Edge. So we based the creative on this AC/DC album cover but in LinkedIn Blue; it was awesome. Campaign numbers and feedback went through the roof. The brand team though had a heart attack. I received a 'talking to' about that.

'Don't hate the media, be the media'

One of the goals of the campaign was to change perceptions of LinkedIn. Facebook was killing it at the time. When Facebook released products, everyone talked about it. If LinkedIn did anything, no one cared. I needed to get people to pay attention to us. The media didn't care about us. Nobody did. So I just decided that if you're marketing on LinkedIn, it's to a 'more sophisticated' audience. Jello Biafra, lead singer of San Francisco punk band the Dead Kennedys famously said: 'don't hate the media, become the media'. We knew nobody else would tell our story so we aimed to do it for ourselves. We started from nothing. When I joined, the marketing solutions blog had 12 subscribers and nine of those were internal. Soon enough we had a couple of hundred thousand subscribers with around 1.5 million unique views. Again, it was all about: 'don't hate the media or the fact nobody's talking about us. Let's tell our own story through our own channels and do our best to amplify and be consistent.' At the start, our LinkedIn company page had maybe 1,500 followers. Now the team has grown it to over 4.5 million – the fastest-growing showcase page in LinkedIn history.

'Be the opposite of everything else'

I used to watch Seinfeld every day when I got off work just to decompress. I love that show. There's a great episode called 'The Opposite' where George Costanza figures out that every decision he makes is wrong, so the opposite must be right. Based on that episode I came up with the most popular blog post I've ever written called 'The George Costanza Approach to Content Marketing'. It listed the 'common marketer's instinct' in a variety of situations and suggested trying the exact opposite. People still talk to me about that blog post.

'You can shrink an arduous sign-off process if the work is good'

I said to my boss, 'give me the numbers you want me to hit', but I had my own agenda. I told him, 'if you want downloads and MQLs, I can get them for you all day long, that's easy. But changing perceptions? Getting people engaged? That's a tougher gig.' However, they didn't ask me to do that. They said, 'get us these MQLs.' So I created the big rocks – The Sophisticated Marketer's Guide – sliced and diced it into 144 different pieces and put it everywhere. Once it started generating 12,000 downloads a month, sales had enough of a pipeline to deal with and demand gen had enough content to fuel their social channels and programmes for months. People left us alone.

The work was so good they were too busy to bother us. That allowed us to free up time to take what CEO Jeff Weiner called 'intelligent risks'.

'Do it yourself'

We would try all sorts of different things. I remember going to my boss and saying: 'I want to do a podcast' and being told 'we don't have the budget for it.' I said: 'Alright, I'll figure out how to do it myself.' It took me a little while, but I launched the podcast, sourced the guests and wrote the questions. I did everything except for the editing. It became a hit. We interviewed [writer] Seth Godin, [Kiss singer and bass player] Gene Simmons and a ton of great marketing leaders. We got used to a 'Do it yourself' ethos. I took up photography at the time as I hated stock photography and all the images in the LinkedIn Library. So I said: 'from now on we're gonna shoot our own.' We started our own photo shoots and using our own art. Instead of 'pretend people' in stock images, we decided we'd only feature real marketers. The marketers in our photos were either in my team, or another LinkedIn team member we'd gotten permission from, or an influencer. Our content starred real people you could follow and connect with.

'If you're a small underdog in a big-budget war you have to work smarter'

We had to be clever about content production. We were up against giants with giant budgets. Take HubSpot. If TikTok launched on a Tuesday, HubSpot would have the 'TikTok Best Practice e-book' fresh in your inbox on Wednesday. We couldn't compete with that. They had more than 40 writers. I had four. Our ethos was: 'IF we're going to make something, it's going to be like an album.' Every piece of copy and every image would be the best you could find anywhere and that's how we'd outgun the market. We had a couple of small boutique agencies, some good friends I'd known for years. We only pushed the best ideas forward. Everything we did was about quality over quantity.

'We were never put off by low numbers if the idea stood up'

I consistently told the team that if a piece of content is good but doesn't work first time, try again. You've got multiple shots at it if the work is good enough. If you believe in the content – a video, whatever it might be – and you launch it but it doesn't do well, change the title; change the cover; change the format if necessary. Relaunch it until it gets the audience it deserves. We were never put off by low numbers. Sometimes we relaunched things three or four times before we got the credit. I trusted that every piece of content we built was based on real insights from our own platform, expert interviews and a little bit of our own passion and hunch. So we knew if we'd put that much work into a piece of content and it failed, it was the messaging, the copy, the creative or the headline that needed changing. It was never the idea that was wrong.

16 No brand, no demand

Somewhere along the line, we've forgotten that we're marketers.

We're so busy choosing marketing tactics and organising our channel strategy that we utterly neglect to invest in building our brands.

Instead, we've opted for accountability over effectiveness. We care less about how well something works than we do about how closely we can track and measure it.

As recently as a few months before I wrote this book, I was on a Zoom meeting with the managing director and leadership team of a very good B2B company. I was responding to a question I'd been asked when the managing director interrupted to 'correct' something I'd said.

'We're not a *brand*,' he told me, 'we're a business.'

This wasn't the first time I'd heard this said by a B2B leader.

When someone declares their company or product is not a brand, I realise the perspective we take for granted as marketers – that your brand is everything you do and say, everything other people think and say about you when you've left the room – is completely alien to other business functions.

It's as if they believe 'brand' to be a term exclusively reserved for say, consumer packaged goods – breakfast cereals, fizzy drinks and tubes of toothpaste.

In the most reductive and base terms I can muster: if you've named a product or service that you sell to customers, how are you not a brand owner?

Doug Kessler, founder of Velocity Partners, asks a better question. 'Why would you *not* want to be a brand?' As he explains:

I'm a huge believer in brand marketing for B2B. I think it's a dramatically undervalued opportunity for every B2B company. And if you don't think you're a brand, the bad news is that you're wrong. You're just a terrible brand.

If you invest no thought into your brand, then by default, your customers are left to perceive you as a fuzzy, nowhere, 'means-nothing' brand. Why would you want that?

Building a strong, spiky, relevant brand with a big, loud point of view doesn't conflict with any other marketing activity you do. It doesn't detract from your demand generation or your account-based marketing. Instead, it *enhances* those activities.

'It's much easier to achieve demand generation if you have a well-established brand,' agrees Margaret Molloy, Siegel+Gale CMO. 'There's far more product and offering in every category than anyone needs. We've too many mail solutions and content management systems to choose from. Brand becomes the true business differentiator when there's over supply.'

Just as it did back in the days of *Mad Men* with washing powder or shampoo, a strong 'brand' can elevate you above competitors and simplify the purchase choice of users.

And yet, for years B2B marketers have neglected to tell the world their stories via big, emotional, personality-driven top of the funnel marketing campaigns.

Why? Because B2B organisations see the use of untargeted messaging and media that doesn't drive rapid, attributable ROI as wasted spend.

As Binet and Field reveal in their research, *The 5 Principles of Growth in B2B Marketing*, that summation is not backed up when studying the patterns common to successful B2B case studies.

The 'centre of gravity' and why brand matters

Margaret Molloy, CMO, Siegel+Gale

Where is the centre of gravity in your organisation? Is it sales? Or perhaps if you work for a B2B tech company the centre of gravity is product?

I don't know that marketing will ever be the centre of gravity in a B2B tech organisation but increasingly, I think brand is. Here's why: historically, the business model for enterprise software was that you bought a big licence with a massive upfront cost. You'd spend a ton of money installing and integrating it as well as an ongoing licence fee.

Now, with cloud software so commonplace, we've transitioned from big, heavy systems to freemium models where you pay only after trying and proving value and need. Then you sign up to a contract that commits you to perhaps 12 months' use.

That shift in business model from a big, one-off deal to an ongoing, long-term relationship with a user – a relationship that's made more fragile with every new market entrant – requires companies to build strong brands.

The market used to be sticky. You chose enterprise software once, installed it and hey presto, you were an 'Oracle Shop' or a 'Microsoft shop'. Now it's less sticky. It's too easy to change platforms.

So suddenly you have to switch your focus from buyers to users – or rather one-off buyers to 'constant buyers'. This has huge implications for your content creation.

Brand plays a role in that shift to a continuous, happy and reassuring relationship that the user is more likely to champion in their communities – in WhatsApp groups and on LinkedIn and Instagram. It's no longer the case that analysts such as Gartner and Forrester are the key information providers on which technologies to buy. B2B has the 'Yelp' factor now. Google and Facebook understand this, as do the newer, emerging giants in Silicon Valley such as Slack and Zoom. These guys do 'brand' extremely well because they understand it as a driver of market share.

The business benefits you miss out on with a weak brand

Peter Field, one of the two renowned marketing effectiveness researchers introduced earlier in the book, hopes the work he and partner Les Binet produced will give B2B marketers the confidence to expend their remit. As he remarks:

> B2B marketers have lacked the evidence and confidence, perhaps, to say to colleagues, 'we need to start thinking about brand marketing'. The data we were able to access for our study performed quite strongly and should be sufficient to convince leaders that the 'bottom of funnel', lead gen activity that B2B marketers have been prioritising is really just 'sales' and lacks real long-term impact.

Field maintains that B2B leaders who reject the idea of investing in a strong brand have failed to see the benefits of doing so even beyond a brand's ability to fuel sales growth.

> A strong brand brings so many other effects to a company. You get to determine your own margins by commanding premium prices. Great brands attract the best people, partners, distributors and suppliers. The ecosystem of benefits that come from having a market-leading brand is enormous.

Rory Sutherland, vice chairman at Ogilvy UK, TED Global speaker and author of *Alchemy: The Surprising Power of Ideas That Don't Make Sense*, makes a similar point and says that when you're famous, luckier things happen to you.

> When my daughters go out on Saturday night, they don't have a specific plan or a measure of success. Nor do they have a set of narrowly defined objectives. The reason they go out is simply that if you put yourself out there, if you're famous or are prepared to meet and become known to lots of people, lucky things are more likely to happen to you.

When you're chief executive of a 'famous brand', he remarks, those 'lucky things' include people returning your call, or your sales executive getting admitted through the door because the person you're targeting wants to hear what they have to say.

'People come to you with business propositions and partnership ideas,' Sutherland continues, 'people want to work for you and sometimes for less money because they want to have a famous brand's name on their CV.'

It's impossible to measure the value of the things Field and Sutherland are describing and also impossible to forecast or predict exactly how or in what order they will play out.

But that doesn't mean it's not worthwhile spending time becoming famous. It just means that when you *are* famous, you'll enjoy advantage of some unspecified kind. And many forms of that advantage will never be quantifiable or directly attributable to the marketing activity you performed.

The vast majority of our B2B organisations are willing to decline those advantages, simply because they can't easily be attributed.

That means the opportunity is doubled for those brave enough to systematically invest in the strength of their brand. The market advantage gained because brand marketing drives long-term growth will be supplemented by the advantage over competitors reluctant to do the same and preferring to measure everything while stagnating.

Having difficulty selling in 'brand'? Get creative...

At Rebeltech, the B2B tech agency that Nicole Lyons and I founded, we used to talk to clients about the advantage of allocating a chunk of their marketing budget towards building brand awareness.

It was never an easy conversation. Even for our clients that invested in their brands and, with the Rebeltech team's help, *benefitted* from it, we still found ourselves having to sell it in repeatedly, week after week.

The unmeasurable stuff makes B2B leaders nervous, *even when it's proving to add demonstrable advantage.*

So we gave our offer a name; we 'branded' what we delivered for our clients. We called it 'targeted brand awareness'. We built a scalable operating system that enabled us to drive the brand 'fame' that we knew would underpin our clients' success, while hitting their specific target communities with relevant content.

At some point, B2B marketing has to let go of its sole reliance on paying only for what it can track, measure and report.

The 'soft' power of brand – the emotional responses that become elevated in your customer engagement – as well as the 'harder' power of brand – the untold commercial value gained – are way too significant not to try.

And it'll take not just trust but actual work.

There will be uncomfortable trade-offs to ensure you're known for the right things, the things that make you different. When you've identified and understood them, they'll point you towards who your customers are but also which prospects and leads you should no longer be chasing.

And you won't just be giving up things in the name of brand awareness. There will be additional activities or content the wider teams outside of marketing need to involve themselves in and play their part in promoting. Brand awareness means a company and its people standing for something and putting themselves out there to prove it. If your brand is going to be built on incredible, 'next-level' customer service, it will require the sales, client and customer success teams to provide daily proof points; to help activate whatever ideas or campaigns you run.

None of this is easy.

Continuing to ignore it, however, is the equivalent of leaving transformative advantage on the table before wondering why your business struggles to scale past the 'closing one or two deals at a time' stage.

17 Find your voice

Who does your brand sound like?

What's its tone of voice?

If you haven't ever stopped to figure this out, it's very possible your marketing materials – your emails, your product one-pagers, your event invitations and your e-books – make you sound like the worst pub evening bore.

Most B2B brands that haven't given tone of voice much thought naturally default to use formal 'business' or C-3PO language full of complicated terms, technical jargon and buzzwords.

Your customer appreciates you keeping your tone simple and friendly. No recipient ever deleted a piece of marketing collateral for being too clear and easy to understand.

There's some thought required in getting your tone of voice sorted. Unless you're so lucky that your company's rare and warm tone of voice just 'evolved' – perhaps a gifted writer in the distant past tried something different and was never questioned – there's work to do.

That work, however, is worth it.

Tone of voice, say experts, is the one and only 'multi-million-dollar weapon' that a marketer wields.

'Voice is huge,' says Doug Kessler of B2B marketing agency Velocity Partners. 'I'm shocked how little it's deployed because it wins markets.'

'A clear, crisp, fun, smart, powerful voice is like a pheromone. It shows confidence; a company that loves what it does and is good at it.'

The reason most companies don't exploit the commercial ammunition that is a warm, frank and even fun tone of voice is that – just as with creativity – they simply don't see it as business-like.

I'll repeat that: *Companies don't see it as business-like... to be friendlier, easier, more appealing for their targets to read, watch and listen to.*

It's not business-like to put target readers at ease? To be more memorable? Or to make them want to devour your next blog or video immediately?

Kessler believes we get too fixated on content in terms of 'what' it says. 'Marketers will obsess like crazy about that but put no energy at all into how they say it.'

Ann Handley, bestselling author and chief content officer at marketing training and education specialist MarketingProfs, notes that tone of voice has the extra benefit of filtering out unprofitable or unsuited prospects you'd rather not work with.

'If your tone of voice works *really* effectively for you,' suggests Handley, 'it can have a secondary benefit in repelling people who wouldn't be a good fit as your customer.'

How do you identify your tone of voice?

There are various ways to go through the process of figuring out how you want your brand to sound in your customers' heads when you speak to them.

Unfortunately, it's going to be hard to avoid creating a style guide of some sort.[17] Sometimes, bravery in B2B marketing will be nothing more than the decision to sound like regular people having a conversation or – even braver – making your language fun, quirky or light-hearted.

Getting to that stage and doing it well, ensuring everybody in your business who writes knows how to strike the right tone, is a complex and labour-intensive process.

---

[17] I say 'unfortunately' because writing a style guide feels (to me at least) like a ball-ache. Some people love doing them. I've worked with superb copywriters who adore the quiet hours spent geeking out over words to create a company's tone of voice 'bible'. If you're a B2B marketer growing a team, find yourself one of these people and employ them immediately. Somebody capable of helping you and your colleagues produce sparkly, imaginative and alluring copy will always be net beneficial to your team's success.

As Handley writes on her website annhandley.com (her blogpost '5 keys to developing a strong tone of voice in your content marketing' is a fine place to start if you consider yourself a beginner):[18]

> *The idea of a style guide might feel pedantic and impenetrable to a lot of businesses—especially growing, scrappy ones who think a style guide is about as appealing as a History of Trigonometric Functions.*
>
> *But a style guide is important for entrepreneurs and small companies, where the brand voice of your organisation grows organically out of the founder's personality and values. That's great. But what happens when the company grows and a marketing team takes over the writing of the emails the founder used to pen herself? That's when you'll be glad you bothered to write all this stuff down.*
>
> *And it's important for larger companies, where content isn't owned by just one or two people. In that scenario, a style guide acts as bumpers on a bowling lane, keeping things on track.*

Get yourself some help

There are countless 'how to write your own style guide' resources online that explain what should go into it but unless you've got specialist copywriting and content people on your team, I advise finding another person to do it with you.

Establishing and documenting your brand's authentic and winning tone of voice isn't something you want to entrust to a merely 'good' writer. There's a YouTube video of Doug Kessler speaking on this; one of the things he says is 'If you only have "good" writers in your business, you need to replace them as soon as possible with "great" writers.'[19]

And when your great writer has completed the piece of work and put your tone of voice to paper, you'll want to take some time working out how to ensure it gets used across every single customer touchpoint. If your style guide is a weighty tome that's left sitting in some desk drawer in the content marketing department, it's not making you money.

The person in your organisation that needs to be responsible for making sure your tone of voice is accessible, understood and used by everybody,

---

[18] A. Handley, '5 keys to developing a strong tone of voice in your content marketing'. Available from https://annhandley.com/5-keys-to-developing-a-strong-tone-of-voice/ [accessed 6 March 2021].

[19] TFM Insights, 'Doug Kessler keynote at TFM&A 2015: Double, treble your budget by mastering tone of voice'. YouTube video, 26 February 2015. Available from www.youtube.com/watch?v=oEruLzPKB2E [accessed 6 March 2021].

is you, the marketing lead. That's right. This opportunity to double or triple your company's revenue is on you. It's as hard as, if not harder than, actually writing a style guide but if you choose to accept this as part of your job and you do it well, you'll instantly be among the very highest-value employees in the business.

Case study: Creative writer Dan Germain

Dan Germain, the man who created and oversaw the copy on the bottle labels of Innocent smoothies, is a brilliant creative who, after the three founders, was probably the most senior figure in the Innocent Drinks business. The Innocent team launched into and shook up a soft drinks category that was ripe for innovation and its products were good. There's no doubt though that Germain's contribution as head of brand and creative was fundamental to the growth of that brand. Coca-Cola now owns the Innocent Drinks company after paying £30m for an 18% stake in 2009 and £76m for a further 38% before buying the rest of the company outright for an undisclosed sum in 2013.

Germain, who has since worked for Apple and now runs Google's Brand Studio as creative director in EMEA, was at Innocent for nearly two decades. His work tone of voice work set the template for that company's culture – he didn't just work on labels but was central to creating the packaging, the ads, the products and everything in-between.

Heavyweight, premium talent and skill embedded into the most senior levels of an outrageously successful business over 20 years: that's the benchmark to look at if you're wondering how much resource you should be committing to your tone of voice.

***

In my home city of Liverpool – I'm from the small town of Southport 20 miles up the coast – a hub for creative and digital startups has emerged in recent years in the industrial area around Jamaica Street. The Baltic Triangle, which sees itself as Liverpool's answer to New York's Meat-Packing District, is home to a copywriter called Dave Harland or, as he's known on social media, Wordman.

Harland is a fierce copywriter with a list of customers all over the world that includes plenty of small and medium-sized businesses as well as the likes of Land Rover, Nespresso, Emirates and MBNA.

Through his newsletter and regular posts on Twitter and LinkedIn he makes fun of himself, tells outrageous stories about made-up characters and acts in his own sketches, all for the sake of capturing eyeballs and drawing attention to his services.

When I've been home to visit family, I've gone to the Baltic Triangle to find Harland, to try to understand how and why he spends so much of his time crafting so much hilarious and often quite zany noise on social media.

'People do ask me why I mess around so much on social media – some don't like it I guess,' admits Harland. 'But every time I post something that feels different to everything else you see on social – and it's different because it's literally me reflecting my unique tone of voice – I get new customers asking for my services.'

Harland agrees with Kessler that tone of voice is the marketing tool that can truly set you apart from your competitors and believes the copywriters needed to achieve that distinction are 'born, not made'.

> I think copywriting can be taught to some extent but the good ones are naturals. It's deep rooted in storytelling which, for me, was a thing from an early age. I was always writing stories and poems; doing work experience at the local newspaper.

Kessler, too, has copywriting in his blood. His father was a copywriter and Kessler grew up interested in advertising. He remembers writing a paper on menthol cigarette advertising at Junior High and recalls family dinners around the table where his father would put a picture up on the fridge and have him and his brothers compete in a caption contest. Such experiences were formative.

Both Kessler and Harland sound gentle warnings about trying to write copy like other admired brands, rather than doing the work to find your own voice. Kessler shares that he's seen clients doing the work of identifying the characteristics that must be represented in their tone of voice. He calls these characteristics 'baselines'.

> I see it all the time where a client insists on having the word 'human' in there. I tell them they can't have it. 'But we want to sound human,' they protest. 'Of course, but I'm asking you to think deeper about who you are. Human is everybody. What other species do you suppose you might otherwise have sounded like?'

That kind of thing is a symptom of brands not taking tone of voice seriously enough, states Harland.

> For so many brands, tone of voice guidelines is a box to tick. They try to go broad. 'You know, we want to be seen as human, warm, friendly. Make us sound like Innocent smoothies.' It reveals how little they know about their own identity or how they want to talk to their customers.

> When I point to excellent or awful examples of copywriting online, I'm trying to help spread a better understanding of this stuff.

Harland's social media feeds are highly recommended among the B2B marketing community for the big but simple learnings he pulls from the copy of what are often deeply unfashionable industries and product categories.

Dave Harland
@wordmancopy

Dear @bannistersfarm, your deliberate omission of the fourth potato, your use of "time's up" instead of "time is up" and your choice of "tucking in" instead of "eating" has made me warm to your brand more.

Here's to the incredible power of #microcopy.

Also, nice spuds!

Here's why former journalists make great B2B marketers
Journalists have skills you can use if your B2B marketing team is going to create brilliant and successful content.

Sure, they can write; we know that. They also understand what makes a story and how to tell it well.

There's a valuable skill, too, in understanding how not to make one's self the story but instead to find someone intrinsically linked with the story topic to interview and make them the hero.

Finally, journalists know instinctively when flexibility is required; when to throw out the plan or the content calendar and respond to events in real time.

There's nothing as fluid and changeable as real life. News moves on and progresses rapidly, often confounding predictions. Journalists understand the story they wrote this morning will evolve again tomorrow, so they're poised for the follow-up. They'll track and write up that story again and again if it's moving fast enough. When you're so used to the goal posts moving like that, you're never wanting for more content or wondering what to write next.

'I believe so strongly in having a background as a journalist,' says Ann Handley, 'because in my mind, journalists think about the customer need like no one else. They've grown up living in their readers' shoes and all the time considering: "how do I simplify and convey this information for the reader?"'

The 'maths' of voice

Earlier in this book, I talked about the importance of having a distinct, compelling story to tell. Now in this chapter you're reading how crucial it is to prioritise tone of voice. How should you think about each and how they fit together? Is one more important than the other?

Doug Kessler has devised a simple mathematical formula (which should please any engineers and product people you might need to engage with on this matter) demonstrating the relationship between the two.

'STORY × VOICE = IMPACT'

The answer to the question above is that you need both. The story and the tone of voice. As Kessler notes:

> I like the multiplication sign part. Anything multiplied by zero is zero, right? So if you have a great tone of voice with all the attitude and everything but nothing to say – well, you've got nothing. And then we've seen the opposite where you've got absolute geniuses with an incredible story but told in such a horrible, dull way that nobody reads it or cares. If you can nail both elements you're on to something.

Case study: GDPR Wars by Path Factory

If you were living anywhere in Europe in 2018, you were subject to the Enormous Boring Email Onslaught that was European businesses responding to the new GDPR rules.

My God, it was hard to get through. Businesses scrambling to bring their opt-ins legally in line with new European consent laws resulted in normal people receiving shedloads of GDPR emails every day.

These emails were covering the driest of topics anyway but, for some reason, brands of every type chose to send them in the same eye-bleedingly dull templates and formats.

Except PathFactory, a content platform for enterprise and mid-market B2B companies, which was clearly very excited about the Star Wars movie release, *Solo: A Star Wars Story*, at around the same time.

PathFactory's email, reproduced in this chapter, performed 241% better than comparable PathFactory email campaigns and won the company a shedload of PR and target audience 'fan-love' on social media.

Tone of voice is huge. Copywriting craft is crucial to doing it well. The value of being distinct and indeed *loved* for the way you speak to your prospects and customers can't be overestimated.

Boring2Brave task

Go and explore your competitors properly, look at their websites, read their descriptions of their products and events. Sign up to their email newsletters. What do you notice? Probably that your market is almost certainly homogenous but maybe also probably quite stale.

How easily could you change things up to stand out?

Customers notice when a company doesn't care enough to sound passionate about what it does.

There's an instinct in me now and again to rage about how we got into a situation where bravery can be demonstrated just by talking like you would to friends; or demonstrating reasons to be excited about the benefits of your widget rather than excited about what's inside and how it works. But here we are.

This is the situation we're in. It's up to us to change it.

An opt-in long ago in an email far, far away...

It is a dark time for B2B. Imperial marketing forces have wrestled control of every prospect's data in the galaxy. Armed with their feared Marketing Automation arsenal, they wield enough power to destroy entire inboxes.

Unknown to the dark side of B2B, rebellious forces have constructed a new hope. A tool for audiences everywhere to take back control of their data and restore freedom to inboxes everywhere. Its name is GDPR.

Here at PathFactory, we are proud members of the GDPR rebellion and pledge allegiance to data transparency, security, and delivering only content that you're interested in for as long as you want to receive it. You can unsubscribe at any time and our Privacy Policy is always available for more details.

So, brave marketer, will you join us in the fight against imperial marketing villainy?

1. Yes! I want to receive all marketing emails from PathFactory

2. Yes, but I only want to receive certain marketing emails from PathFactory

18 Fast and slow: Mastering two-speed marketing

When I left my job helping to run a small group of PR and marketing services companies at a global communications network and joined SaaS personalisation software company Qubit, it was my first taste of a B2B tech startup and scale-up environment. I was blown away at how fast everything moved.

It was amazing. Ideas that would have taken traditional PR agencies maybe two months to be honed, signed off and executed took Qubit's young marketing talent half a day.

You want some promotional collateral for the event that you just pitched to your boss in the 9am meeting? Sure.

By lunchtime, the creative guys could have a series of high-quality video shorts integrated through HubSpot and drawing attention through targeted YouTube ads.

Strategy discussions didn't always wait for meetings; conversations with the CEO out on the floor or in a stairwell could change the direction you'd been heading in and set you firing off on another course. It was fun but, at times, insane.

The necessity to solve problems at speed and work in real time was one of the things I'd loved as a daily newspaper journalist and had missed since I left that profession.

This new startup environment gave me that but also the added allure of a steep learning curve and the sweet feeling of working with some of the smartest people I'd ever met.

I was hooked.

When you work in a startup environment, that speed is like a drug. It's like nothing else in corporate or business life.

Alexander Von Schirmeister knows what I mean. A former eBay CMO, Von Schirmeister has also worked for corporate giants Procter & Gamble, Telefonica and RS Components.

In September 2019, he joined payments startup SumUp and like me when I started at Qubit, was captivated by the rapid 'can do' mentality:

> Yeah I'm loving it. It's very different to anything I've done in the past. You communicate very differently on Slack than you do by email. The speed of information distribution is very different compared to a larger, legacy company.
>
> In the past, we would typically grab hold of a project and take it away before coming back with recommendations. And you bring back a recommendation which then works its way up to the board for approval.
>
> In a startup, someone fires up a Google Doc and before you know it, 20 people are co-authoring it. You're thinking: 'This is madness. Just delegate. Give it to me, I'll take it away and bring it back.'
>
> But that's not the way the new generations of talent work. You could argue whether it's the best way but it does bring about dialogue and open conversation that in other companies just doesn't happen. Ultimately, it also leads to much faster decision making. The decisions are being made right there in the document.

Von Schirmeister notes that there is a vast cultural divide between legacy companies and startups when it comes to attitude, risk appetite, tools and processes.

I tell Von Schirmeister though that I've come full circle in some respects. I love the speed at which startups can do business and create new opportunity. Von Schirmeister is correct. It really is the way younger people want to work and they're so naturally adept with technology that they don't see why they'd accept anything more cumbersome.

On the other hand, and perhaps ironically, a great deal of time is wasted when working at that breakneck speed. You can find yourself going back and forth over old ground with constant changes in direction. You can end up spending excessive amounts of money creating or putting out work that hasn't properly been thought through and on its release isn't even close to being finished.

The discipline and craft, the understanding of positioning and the diligent care taken in properly communicating a plan – all of which you'd find in the likes of Von Schirmeister's former workplaces – is starkly absent in most startup HQs.

Sometimes you have to slow things down to speed them up. Spreading yourself thin over hundreds of different marketing channels often isn't as clever as reducing the number of those channels and making a genuine impact.

If the ultimate goal of a B2B marketing campaign is simply to capture hundreds of thousands of eyeballs, then sure, keep spinning the wheel and churning out massive volumes of rubbish. If, however, you want to capture your prospects' hearts, minds and budget, there has to be some nod to genuine craft and focus.

It takes time and thought to create work that's meaningful and memorable; to make it shareable; to make it distinct; to just make it better. Von Schirmeister agrees: 'There's definitely a happy medium here. SumUp went for someone like me in the first place because they wanted someone with grey hair to come in and help them be more mature and process driven.'

'Perfect' marketing versus an 'MVP mindset'

Von Schirmeister also makes the very good point though that startups – born largely from a product and technology bias rather than a commercial or marketing bias – exist with an 'MVP (minimum viable product) mindset'.

> It's about pushing products out as fast as possible. The notion of MVP means it doesn't matter if what we push out is embarrassingly bad – the sooner we put something embarrassing out and get market feedback, the sooner we can get it right.

He argues that mindset puts paid to the idea of 'perfect marketing'.

> At P&G or at eBay, we'd test the campaign until the cows come home before we actually shot it. You would test a storyboard repeatedly. Nobody's going to commit money to expensive creative production or a large media buy until we're sure. Nowadays marketing can be lighting up a couple of keywords on Google. The barrier to entry for marketing is so miniscule. That's why so much attention maybe goes into a product and not marketing.

Von Schirmeister agrees though that for marketing to work, it has to live up to its name. 'Marketing still has a massive role to play. Demand generation is the easy part. Building a brand and a company takes time and skill.'

Do you sit near your company's GSD-er?

Beware anyone who spends a few seconds of every meeting telling everyone else: 'I'm a "get shit done" kind of person.'

It sounds appealing to have a 'get shit done' person on your team, right?

Most of us would hear that description and love to be known as a 'get shit done' person.

Sadly, the description (like so much bad marketing) often hides trouble.

'GSD' people can be toxic. They often dislike detail, planning and process and they groan at having it suggested to them that they slow down and work with the rest of their team on the task in hand. Craft, quality and original thought – these things mean little to most GSD-ers.

The biggest problem with GSD-ers though is not that they are annoying (although they can be), but that they measure their impact and success in shit.

They boast about delivering shit and because volume, rather than quality of activity, is what means most to them ('Folks, I'm going to miss this meeting because I've got something else I need to do'; 'This needs to be actioned now'; 'I reckon that shouldn't take you any more than 15 mins...'), shit is exactly what comes out.

They often work in isolation of any agreed plan or strategy and are experts at spreading confusion. I've seen them spend money without bothering to be accountable and they invariably deliver what they say they will, and produce shit-quality work.

GSD-ers shy away from collaboration. They like to delegate but don't share. They don't see any value in winning people's support or gathering the buy-in needed to make an idea real.

Frequently, by the time their shit starts to stink, they're two or three projects on and have wiped their hands clean of responsibility.

What follows is a real conversation I recently had with a GSD-er. I was a consultant. Her boss was my direct client but I was involved with other workflows, owned by several of her colleagues. I'd also started looking after the other consultants the client company was using for digital and content marketing – we'd got into a pretty good groove as a team.

> **GSD-er:** *I want a marketing meeting with you and the team to let you know how you can help me.*
>
> **Me:** *Sure thing. We actually already have a couple of weekly marketing meetings with the management team. Do you want to join those? There's a lot going on so it would be good to feed your workflows into the bigger plan to make sure we're all aligned.*
>
> **GSD-er:** *No. I want my own marketing meeting. I don't care about all the things you're discussing in the other meeting and I don't have the time for talking. I just want to get shit done. I'm a get shit done kind of person. That's why I'm frustrated*

that I haven't heard back from you on the brief I sent you last week. It feels like we're drifting.

Me: I understand, but we do report to (her boss) who's agreed a budget against certain goals and deliverables that everyone is now aware of. I actually sought to get the things you and I talked about off the ground, but it hit an impasse because the management team is split between what you're asking for and what others want. That's why it would be great if you joined the marketing meeting so you can present to the whole team.

GSD-er: Those meetings don't work for me.

Me: Well, we need to get your ideas in front of the leadership team somehow and we'll need to check in with the CFO on budget as well so...

GSD-er (interrupts): We've got money – what we don't have is time. I know what I'm doing – I've been doing this for a long time and I'm known for my success. I can throw money at the problem if you start moving forward. I love what (a direct competitor and the largest global player in the market) has done – let's do that.

Me: Yes, it's pretty good. But they're a different brand with a different promise and they've obviously got budgets we don't have. [Her boss] asked us to differentiate and shake things up as a new entrant remember? We can be beaten on scale and price but we really can differentiate on message and positioning.

GSD-er: Yes but I don't care about differentiation. At least they're actually doing something. I want to do something.

Me (knowing I'm getting nowhere and so resorting to tried-and-tested 'consultancy pandering'): Here's what I suggest. You're the experienced one here. You've done this hundreds of times. Come into the group marketing meeting and share with us the things that have always worked for you before – those brilliant gems you'd never want to lose that we can build around?

GSD-er: I haven't got time to write your marketing strategy for you...

And so on.

There's a very bright halo that sits above the head of anyone in B2B marketing (and particularly tech startups) who has a reputation for getting things done fast and moving on. Speed is good, as is agility and the use of technology to make decision making accessible to all. But B2B marketers looking to increase impact and influence should be wary of joining the glorification of speed over quality. Ten poor-performing pieces of marketing produced in a fortnight doesn't come close to matching the value of a brilliantly insightful idea that sales colleagues can feast on for an entire quarter.

The big, black hole where proper segmentation should be

This isn't an exact science – it certainly doesn't speak to all companies on either side of the fence – but if we could bottle the real-time responsiveness, agility and sheer energy of the fast-growth, agile startups together with the storytelling craft of the big corporates, would we have perfect B2B marketing?

Not quite, suggests Professor Mark Ritson, who manages and teaches the *Marketing Week* mini-MBA. He comments that there also has to be a discussion about the modern B2B marketer's understanding of the difference between strategy and tactics.

> *The process is missing. So the minute B2B marketers jump to tactics, which most of them do immediately, all is lost anyway.*

> *Proper segmentation is the killer difference in B2B. So you've either built a segmentation of the whole market and identified different segments where you want to play and where you don't; or you haven't. That's something B2B sales teams rarely recognise. Instead, they target everyone.*

> *The minute you build a decent segmentation as a B2B marketer, you will have just tripled or quadrupled the opportunity for the sales team because they're able to focus.*

When that level of segmentation is in place, Ritson observes, you can get into 'positioning' and only then 'tactical execution', 'but,' he adds, 'you don't see that many cases of decent B2B segmentation, even though it isn't rocket science.'

As well as lacking a proper segmentation, Matthew Robinson of Contentsquare says he's surprised how few B2B marketers actually build a proper plan before the year starts. Robinson's team is responsible for half of Contentsquare's revenue target, so at the end of each year Robinson lists all the different activities he's planning the following year and attributes a conservative number of leads that he'll target per activity.

Boring2Brave task

What does a good marketing plan look like?

Mark Ritson agrees on the need for a proper marketing plan. Here, he details the process behind it and what it should incorporate.

★ Without a marketing plan everything turns into tactics. So agree a planning approach whereby you get your marketing proposal in front of the senior team to say: 'This is what we want to do next year...'

★ Figure out when your 'planning season' is for the following year and begin early. Encourage others across the organisation to look at the marketing plan as early and often as possible.

★ Calendars and dates are purely the tactical part. Certainly, a decent marketing plan would have that – something at the end that shows what's going to happen and when. But preceding that is all the segmentation and positioning work, the targeting and rationale; the initial research showing who you're going after and why.

★ After the chart with your dates and calendar, there's a budget proposal showing how much money you want to invest in marketing this year and what the incremental return will be.

Multi-dimensional marketing

In early-stage startups, the ratio of salespeople to marketers can be as many as 6:1. Each of those salespeople has a legitimate demand on your time and focus.

How do you create the number of campaigns or pieces of content that will speak to all of their needs, for each sales conversation they're having on any given day?

That's before we consider the regular and varied demands on you as a marketer from your CEO, your COO or commercial director and others – HR or the head of product marketing and so on.

It's impossible. There isn't enough time in your week. So what do you do instead? You probably float around trying to multi-task, organising your time to the very minute, trying to add specks of value to each of them, constantly prioritising demands by their level of urgency or, if you're smart, which of your 'internal clients' has the power to fire you.

In reality, by trying to meet all their needs with separate activities, you're affecting nothing.

And even if you are, when was the last time one of those sales reps publicly thanked you for your contribution to 'their' success in closing a huge deal? When did a salesperson stand at the front of an all-hands meeting to take the applause before admitting that they couldn't have done it without you?

The only recognised measure of how valuable you are to those sales conversations is the speed and appetite with which the salesperson comes back to you next time to see what ideas and activities you might contribute to their next deal.

And here's the thing – that could be a blog, a white paper or a webinar. It might be no more than just a channel of distribution or a story with a single focus – one industry sector for one hungry sales executive.

If you're going to contribute value that is widely recognised internally, however, it's far more likely to be a 'multi-dimensional' idea or insight that transcends individual industry sectors and elevates the business above competitors' chatter. It will make for a story big enough – like Jason Miller's 'big rock' – to feed the next three months' worth of brilliant content. In that way, it's going to have so much more value to so many colleagues trying to sell the product and indeed the brand.

How to come up with a multi-dimensional marketing idea

B2B marketers don't just face the challenge that they have too many people to 'serve'; they also have seemingly limitless channels to manage. This is especially prevalent in the B2B tech sector where expectations on you are higher due to your colleagues' extreme level of comfort with technology.

B2B marketing seems often to feel like an endless race to complete as many different activities as you can.

As an experiment though, one suggested by Doug Kessler at Velocity Partners, why not take the budget for the next five pieces you've planned and choose to put it behind one 'great' piece. It's hard to think that way when there's so much to do and when every individual senior leader and sales colleague is used to asking you to service their own 'personal' marketing needs. It's harder still when you admit that this one great thing may not work.

If you can convince the powers that be though and make it work, it should demonstrate to your organisation how effective marketing can be if you have time to plan and build something with weight and quality.

A multi-dimensional marketing idea – one that can serve your distinct market positioning while acting as an umbrella idea under which all your relevant content and stories can hang – should be as broad as possible.

A previous client of mine at Rebeltech has a technology that helps parcel delivery businesses find the right front door with more speed and accuracy than Google Maps and other proprietary technologies. Rather than focusing on selling the product, we built and sustained a content-driven private online community called the Last Mile Consortium. The group consisted of enterprise brands, logistics and delivery operators and tech vendors in the ecommerce space. The breadth of the theme enabled us to drive content, PR, events and ABM that covered endless topics, challenges and issues that were universally felt across the industry. The constant conversation was hosted, facilitated and 'owned' by our client, who benefitted from the network with several high-profile enterprise deals.

If we'd dived into the client brief above in the normal, agile and real-time way that startup marketing tends to work, we would have probably tried to look for some PR stories to pitch to journalists. Only by slowing down to think were we able to come up with the Last Mile Consortium – an alluring and powerful global online community of industry insiders looking to work together to solve problems. Conversations, partnerships and deals that all led back to our client.

19 Technology versus talent

B2B marketing adores process and worships at the holy altar of measurability. We just love counting stuff. Basically, if you can measure it – it's a go-er.

As a side effect of making everything so much easier, the technologies that have taken marketing far beyond where any of us imagined they would have asserted the 'science' aspect of marketing over the 'art'.

As discussed in this book at length already, the problem with this is that the things that stand to make B2B marketing brilliant – bravery, brand focus and creativity – can't be counted. Creativity itself is unreliable, imprecise, difficult to forecast *before* you deploy it and wholly unmeasurable *after*.

Bravery, at least, is scalable. Bravery breeds. One brave act inspires another. Creativity isn't at all scalable. There's no formula. Nothing you can put in a spreadsheet to predict an outcome. This makes it awkward to discuss with colleagues who like everything to be neat and tidy.

Creativity can be key to unlocking outrageous commercial success in a way counting can't. That most of us B2B marketers struggle to work with the unpredictable is at least part of the reason why the few that do are sensationally successful and so far out of their competitors' reach.

The 'tech versus talent' trajectory we're on

In November 2018, marketing hit an interesting milestone. For the first time, according to a report published by the analyst Gartner, chief marketing officers were allocating a greater proportion of their budgets to technology than people.[20]

Gartner's report surveyed senior marketing executives across the US and UK and found that marketing technology expenditure that year climbed from 22% to 29% while staff costs headed in the opposite direction, dropping from 27% to 24% over the same period.[21]

Peter Field, one of the two researchers along with Les Binet who shone new light on what makes for effective B2B marketing in 2019, argues that creativity has been 'murdered' by short-term thinking twinned with digital technology:

> There's been immense, untold damage done to creativity by 'short-termism'. We're faced with an increasingly digital agenda of rapid 'Wham-bam, thank you, ma'am' type marketing. It's utterly disposable but generates fantastic ROI because no money is spent behind it. We're killing creativity.

We should resist any temptation to pit the enormous capability of new technologies against the human brain's capacity for genius, creative moments and instead explore how all these elements of B2B marketing could work together.

An example: if we're going to employ 50% of our budget on technology that enables incredible automation and efficiencies of operations, where is the logic of promoting people with a talent for process and operations up the marketing hierarchy?

For a long while, it's looked increasingly likely that future CMOs would predominantly come from a computer science background. For sure, those skills are needed within the marketing function. But given the constant emergence of new, powerful and easy-to-use technologies, how much does it benefit the business for marketing to be led by someone who sees the world through the lens of digital performance and analytics? Could the complementary skills of strategic creativity and storytelling be more usefully promoted to ensure organisations with the same data as their competitors are able to cut through with more insight-led campaigns to compete?

---

[20] Gartner, 'CMOs spend more on technology than talent', 9 November 2018. Available from www.gartner.com/en/marketing/insights/articles/cmos-spend-more-on-technology-than-talent [accessed 6 March 2021].
[21] An interesting aside: the 'top' technology priorities noted in the Gartner research were email marketing, online management and digital analytics but those priorities were expected to shift in future towards artificial intelligence, which 'might one day design marketing campaigns instead of people'.

The seven traits found in every B2B CMO

Fiona Jensen is a specialist recruiter with 17 years' experience in placing B2B marketers in roles for a host of top businesses. She also created the Market Mentors podcast, which featured her interviewing a stack of B2B marketing leaders from across the world and uncovering hundreds of great tips for job seekers. Here, she lists the ingredients she's seen present in all the CMOs and leaders she's worked with.

1.   **A learning mindset:** Everyone that I met who reached a senior level all had 'learning mindsets'. They're never done. There's always something new; always a new platform to master or a new trend to explore.

2.   **Humility:** Every CMO was very modest about the fact that they don't know it all.

3.   **Curiosity, readers of everything:** Everyone's a reader. Every single one of them. I'm not just talking about books, it could be magazines. It could be specific websites, but they all have a habit of reading deeply in subject matter. So whether it's relative to the market sector they're in, their hobbies and interests, the job, the required tools of the job or, you know, just general literature. And all of them are heavy readers. You'd ask them that one question: 'what do you like to read?' and the lists would appear, as long as your arm. All of them seek inspiration from elsewhere.

4.   **Great stealers:** I don't know whether you know that sort of 'steal like an artist' approach, but many of the leaders I talk to and work with are modest in talking about the fact that they're not reinventing the wheel. What they do instead is look at what works, where and how it works and whether it can be applied to their own scenario or situation.

5.   **People-centric:** They're all massively 'people people'. They're generous with their time and with their advice. They're very quick to understand a request and say a firm 'yes' or 'no', so they have a fast decision-making thing going on; a sort of 'test and fail fast' approach.

6.   **Communicators:** They're all very good communicators. They leave you in no doubt how they feel about something – whether they know or they don't know, or how they plan to approach something.

7.   **Generous:** There's a real problem-solving generosity thing at work in the people I'd call leaders. A lot of them have come up with their own workflows, worksheets, templates for bits of processes which they then supply freely to the rest of the team, company or community. They instinctively like to make things easy for other people.

Not one of these traits, identified in marketing leaders by an experienced B2B marketing recruiter, speaks to a particular ability with regard to technology. They are all far more anthropological in essence. That's not to say of course that marketing leaders comfortable with data and tech aren't increasingly well equipped to do the job; it's simply noting that such a skill doesn't fall into this headhunter's 'must have' list of CMO characteristics.

***

When Andrew Logan, founder of digital marketing agency and HubSpot specialist Floww, finished university with a degree in marketing in 2006, he was left feeling disappointed and thoroughly unprepared for the world of work.

'It was just before Facebook really took off and probably only about two years after Google really became prevalent,' says Logan.

'We were basically chucked out of this old-fashioned marketing machine at the end of the course, into a new world that seemed to have little resemblance to anything we'd studied.'

Logan got a job on the floor of a fashion retail store to give himself the time to spend his nights mastering digital marketing with the help of various online courses. That blend of self-taught digital expertise and 'real-world' commerce, he says, served him well.

> I think quite often and as marketers we pigeon-hole ourselves and say 'I'm the social guy' or 'I'm the performance guy'. When we were starting out at Floww and getting people on board to help out, we talked to so many people who knew their way around social media platforms like the back of their hand. They knew how to push the buttons but they didn't know why they were pushing them or what mattered. They would point to big campaigns and say 'look at all the likes and shares I got'. But I'd look at it from my small business background and saying: 'Right, but what about sales? What about profit? What problem did you help solve?'

There's no doubting the incredible impact that the proliferation of technology and automation has had on our capability as businesses and especially marketing. We're in a supremely privileged position compared to any previous generation of marketers. The size of the potential for even greater capacity demands that we continue to investigate how far technology can help us reach.

But equally, I'd argue that the cheap availability of automated tools has impacted on our hunger and commitment to develop our skills and instincts as marketers and business people.

Logan observes:

> If we were being reductive about digital marketing channels you'd say they are just delivery channels – the smart-bombing delivery system helping us invent new and brilliant ways to get your message out.
>
> But the copy and the positioning, the strategic brand-building stuff that aligns to business goals and helps your organisation generate trust – nobody will buy you without those things.

Logan's remarks reflect why all of us are hammered with promotional emails every day that we never bother to open. I mean, sure, congratulations to the sender for getting in front of your target recipient but commiserations on the bland email subject headers that make you so sadly and speedily irrelevant.

Scott Brinker, VP Platform Ecosystem at HubSpot and editor of leading marketing technology blog chiefmartec, often gets asked for his view on the perfect 'martech stack'.

> It's a funny thing, people get really hung up on the perfect stack. 'What's the perfect tool for me?' The reality is the tool matters less than you'd think. If I have a crappy tool but I use it really well, I will outperform someone who spent a ton of money on some state-of-the-art machine but has no idea how to use it to solve problems for customers.
>
> If I went to Home Depot and picked up the most expensive power tools to build a deck in my yard. I assure you, it's gonna be an absolute friggin' disaster. My father-in-law though, who's talented in this regard, could probably come over with a beat-up hammer and saw and make something amazing. It's the talent not the tool.

As marketers, we're becoming tech experts but we need to look back to the original purpose of the marketing discipline and rediscover our status as customer experts. If we continue on the road towards our role beginning and ending with attaining MQLs to give to a sales guy, we risk killing marketing within a generation.

20 Brief braver

I believe B2B companies could improve their marketing output ten-fold immediately just by learning to brief better.

In all my time working for startups and scale-ups, I can count the number of marketing and communications briefs I've seen on one hand with fingers to spare.

The tasks you're set as an in-house marketer or marketing agency in those environments generally come down to three things.

1   Get us more leads.

2   Get us some PR.

3   Help us raise money/find a buyer.

Often there's little more detail given than that.

None of those things is a real brief. A brief should articulate, among other things, a problem that needs solving. The brief would implicitly ask the question: 'how can you employ marketing and communications to help me solve this problem?'

None of the three needs above articulate a problem. Instead, they're someone presenting you with the answer and asking you to go and execute on it.

As a marketer, I'd like to hear the question or the problem. In the case of instruction number 1 ('Get us more leads'), the problem might actually be: 'We've got an excellent product that beats all of the competitors in our space but we struggle to close deals so we need more leads in the pipeline to give us a chance of making a sale.'

The solution to that problem might be any number of things, including but not exclusively:

- ★ lower your prices;
- ★ *raise* your prices;
- ★ change your sales training with a focus on closing;
- ★ reframe or redraft your market positioning;
- ★ and so on.

A brief is useful to the marketer or marketing agency but is just as useful, if not more so, to the wider business. Writing a decent brief helps define the problem you're trying to solve and adds the context of the specific factors and challenges you face.

In a 2010 article for *adliterate*, Saatchi & Saatchi chief strategy officer Richard Huntington wrote a note to clients to explain how they could write more inspiring briefs.[22]

Huntington shares examples of great briefs – none of them solutions; each of them problems. He writes: 'Advertising agencies are problem solving companies, albeit that they solve commercial problems by applying creativity to the task.'

Huntington offers the following real briefs as examples of problems or challenges that he feels could be better solved with creativity:

- ★ T-Mobile – take the lion's share of the £30+ monthly contract market.
- ★ Teenage binge drinking – reduce the harm that comes to young people when they drink too much.
- ★ Police recruitment – attract quality recruits to the Metropolitan Police by making 999 out of 1000 people realise they could never be a Police Officer.

When we as B2B businesses get used to seeing our problems as open-ended questions rather than 'an already accepted solution' in need of delivery, we'll begin to understand the vast potential of what marketing can achieve for us.

When you're writing a brief – whether it's to inform your recruiter on the ideal job spec for the hire you need to make or whether you're briefing your creative agency on the goals of the next campaigns – start afresh each time. It'll force you to think.

It's the easiest thing in the world to start with an old brief and 'update' the old copy. Creative director, copywriter and author Dave Trott says:

---

[22] R. Huntington, 'Creating inspiring briefs – a note to clients'. Adliterate, 10 May 2010. Available from www.adliterate.com/2010/05/creating-inspiring-briefs-a-note-to-clients/ [accessed 6 March 2021].

'People are always looking for formulas because they don't understand the difference between formulas and principles. Put simply, with a principle you have to use your brain, with a formula you don't. Which is why lazy people prefer formulas.'

'Greatness is rarely in the brief...'

Doug Kessler, creative director, comments that few B2B budget owners would actually recognise great marketing. They're not aiming for it because they don't know what it would look like.

> Greatness is rarely in the brief. From the start, there's just no ambition. It's not like people are missing the target. They're not even trying. They're just trying to do something that credibly looks like what other people call marketing because that's what non-marketers and mediocre ones do.

To help B2B budget owners brief better, marketing agencies in the space could reinvent themselves as masters in the solution of problems, just as Huntington describes advertising agencies above.

Ogilvy vice chairman Rory Sutherland agrees, believing B2B agencies should trade on their ability to make breakthroughs for their clients 'through perceptual understanding as opposed to objective understanding':

> Whether something sells or not is not a product of what it is but a product of how you sell it: the context in which you frame it; the competitive set you choose for it; how you price it and not only how you price, but how you describe the pricing because procurement is engaged in a framing exercise.

When Ogilvy pitched to a global satellite network owner and operator, a classic B2B tech business, the agency framed discussion of its fee in a very clever way. Instead of saying: 'our monthly fee is X thousand pounds', the agency told the satellite maker: 'our monthly fee is equal to the cost of fuel needed to get one of your rockets the first 110 feet in the air from the launch pad.'

'We made the cost of the agency's expertise seem so irrelevant in the scheme of what the client was doing as to make it little more than a rounding error,' shares Sutherland.

I'm certain that introducing the discipline of writing solid briefs ahead of a campaign or activity would have a transformative effect on B2B marketing's capacity for driving true commercial advantage.

At the very least it would demand fuller conversations and a deeper understanding within organisations of the various elements of marketing and the relationships they have with one another.

Imagine an organisation, for example, that sells a very good product far too cheaply to customers and can't figure out the way to charge more. Without framing the problem in a creative marketing brief, months are spent training the sales team to try and squeeze more out of customers who have too many alternative options to choose from. More time then goes by as the product team comes under pressure to deliver incremental innovation in lieu of market differentiation and value. All this time the problem remains.

Give the same problem to an experienced marketer to solve and the answer might come in the form of another question: 'What do our customers think we do?'

And another question: 'Does it seem to a new prospect like we understand where their business is heading? Do we feel like the sort of partner they *need* to be associated with?

And another: 'Have we given our prospects *any* reason to buy us other than our relatively low price and our product features that are more or less the same as our competitors'?'

The CEO is all ears but on hearing the marketer's subsequent proposal that the company creates market FOMO and competitive advantage through thinking about how to build a premium brand, he/she recoils. 'Too long a process, too expensive and there's no guarantee it will work.'

And so the company continues believing the problem to be solvable through driving more out of beleaguered sales and product teams. I'll bet you've been witness to this scenario or something similar a number of times. I know I have.

Now, instead, imagine if marketing departments worked at the front end of problem solving, and B2B businesses relied upon them to reframe the questions and offer psychological or, as Sutherland puts it, 'perceptual' fixes instead of 'objective' ones.

I'm not crazy. I know how far away and unlikely this will sound to many of you – not just in B2B but across all businesses. But if bosses were used to approaching their most creative people with questions rather than answers, I believe a huge number of the tough, intangible business problems we *all* struggle with would get solved and disappear.

And that understanding – that habit of asking questions rather than prescribing the answers – it begins with a good brief.

21 Building 'brand' bridges: 'Coffee and shoe leather'

I worked for a man who'd learned his trade as a marketing manager for one of the world's top five brands. He had superb knowledge, was incredibly driven and about as intelligent a person as I've ever met.

But I was told by a number of people across the company we worked for that they never bothered opening his emails. These weren't company or group emails being ignored. They were personally addressed emails about ongoing projects.

I found it a pretty shocking thing to hear. It didn't reflect at all well on the people who told me.

When I asked why, the reason given to me was always the same complaint: 'He emails so often with new requests but then follows up on them so infrequently that it doesn't seem to matter whether we read them or not. Meanwhile, we've got our own jobs to do.'

What they said was partly true. This man was known for his constant ideas, many of them great ones. What he somehow neglected was to take the time to sell them properly.

Pretty much anything you try to do in an organisation that's at all worthwhile requires you to build a coalition of support. To change anything for the better requires you to borrow the time and actions of others. To do this you need to be persuasive and personable. People skills are vital.

It's hard to be brave as a team of one…

Most of the B2B experts I spoke to for this book cited building up a community of internal champions among the most critical factors of success in B2B marketing.

This counts double if you're going to start asking for permission to do things that are out of the norm. Before you attempt to revolutionise marketing and show your organisation what brave marketing can do, before you try to carry that flag up the hill, you have to find people to do it with you.

'I don't know how brave you can be as a team of one,' agrees Ann Handley, bestselling author and chief content officer at MarketingProfs:

> You've got to pull people along with you, your colleagues and the C-suite because you can't be a lone soldier out there. You won't be effective unless you articulate to others why it's important to be brave. The more consensus you build, the more wins you're able to show, the more people you'll get in your corner and the more confidence you'll have, which is another foundation for bravery.

As my former manager discovered, emails aren't the best way to get busy colleagues to do what you need them to.

To wield influence, you have to be a relationship builder. However you do it best, that's the way it needs to be done.

For me, it's always been a coffee and shoe leather thing. I reckon I've spent about a quarter of my career walking around various floors or common areas of my office buildings chatting to people at their desks or over coffees.

Most of the time we're talking shop. Other times not. It's a useful way to grow your understanding of other people's jobs and how all our responsibilities and priorities fit together. You sometimes find ways to work together to solve problems you otherwise wouldn't have known existed.

Most of all though, while you grow friendships and influence, you get to spread a little subtle PR about the work the marketing team is doing. This stuff helps more than any seniority or decrees from above when you need to pull in their help for your ideas and campaigns.

If a busy person is going to stretch their already long day to share their time and brains, it's going to be because they want to. It won't be because they've been ordered to.

Margaret Molloy, CMO of Siegel+Gale, feels that any opportunity for B2B marketers to improve their own PR is a positive:

> Ironically, I think some B2B marketers are the worst at marketing and promoting marketing internally. Shame on us that we're not persuasive enough to successfully evangelise the merits of the craft.

What do you think would be the response if you were to show greater interest in the conversations adjacent to those B2B marketing traditionally concerns itself with?

You already work closely with sales but there are elements of product, pricing, distribution and customer feedback that could all benefit from a grown-up conversation about linking the power of the brand to the wider business.

Nobody needs to give you a pay rise or a title bump for you to start elevating brand and marketing from an internal reputation for being tactics-driven, to a more strategic realm.

Molloy is correct. The more reasons you can find to collaborate with other functions the better. Take segmentation. Rather than building it in isolation, Professor Mark Ritson suggests a powerful approach to reinforcing an important relationship:

Go to your best contact on the sales team and say: 'look, I'm building the segmentation. Can you help me? Here's the model I'm using. Does this feel right to you?'

You can always tell a decent B2B marketer because a couple of the sales team come along when they present a marketing plan. It means that the sales team want the plan, that they believe in the plan.

The more a sales team believes in and trusts your plan, the less they're likely to intrude and disrupt your plan throughout the year.

Marketing skills versus ability to influence

Ritson shares that when it comes to succeeding in B2B marketing, he'd actually trade in a team's marketing skills for the ability to build relationships.

I'd absolutely swap B2B marketing competence for the ability to interact with and influence the sales team.

Let's say you've got a really good technical marketer. He's eight out of ten in terms of capability but the sales guys think he's an idiot and he has one out of ten in terms of influence. When you multiply those two factors out he scores only 8% potential.

Then you take a less technically good marketer, maybe a six out of ten. But she's pretty good on influencing and interacting with the sales team. Maybe she's an ex-salesperson herself. Give her a six for influence and suddenly she's at 36% potential.

You look for one of the key skills of a B2B marketer being the ability to manage relationships across the sales and the other functions, to involve them in strategy and keep them onside.

If you're not at the top of your organisation or function, then a big part of your job becomes finding and nurturing the stakeholders who can give you cover and support your efforts when needed. You have to earn that support and respect in the internal marketplace.

Some of your success will be based on your ability to devise and sell in ideas and strategy, but a big chunk of it will come down to your own credibility in the company. Do you have that credibility? Have you built respect for the things you're good at?

If the answer is yes, that comes with all sorts of advantages. You're listened to; sought out for your opinion and help; you've got support in every function. It gives you a licence to operate.

If the answer's no, there's some fixing to do. If you don't have internal influence, then you're stuck with the status quo; change is beyond you.

'If a marketer is just doing marketing in his own little bubble and not working shoulder to shoulder with the sales team, he'll fail,' notes Ritson. 'B2B marketers have to engage the sales team to help and work with them. You know the old joke, "almost as if they worked for the same company"'.

The onus is mostly on us marketers to find a way to get things operating well. It will never be the job of the salesperson, simply because he or she will always be able to demonstrate his or her value through deals closed.

We have to do that while not becoming beholden to every last whim of each salesperson. The job is not to give away our power but to build relationships on mutual respect and need and with an expectation of mutual wins.

Repairing a poor predecessor's reputation: Do it now for those who come after you

Ritson's view is that we are starting out from a bad place because of the poor standard of B2B marketing that preceded us.

> To be fair to the sales teams and the rest of the organisation, in most B2B companies they've had to deal with total rubbish from previous marketing teams.
>
> If I was a CFO and I'd lived through the typical marketing bullshit most 50-year-old CFOs have, you'd expect me to be cynical by this point.
>
> What they've encountered before is such toss that they're assuming you're probably as bad as everyone else has been. So a good B2B marketer has to go in and, before anything else, engage them in a way that says: 'I'm going to help you

make money here. But, you have to give me a few things in return; we have to work together on this.'

The job of marketing is teaching, not having great ideas

Doug Kessler, founder and creative director of Velocity Partners, discusses the importance of teaching in marketing:

> I spent too much of my career thinking that having great ideas was my job and that people would instinctively just see they were good ideas and get out of my way.
>
> And if they didn't, that was an obstacle and I'd get frustrated. It took me way too long in my career to realise 'that's not an obstacle, that's my job.'
>
> The job is getting people on board with what you are trying to do. What are the chances that their idea of what great marketing for this company looks like would be exactly the same as yours? There's no chance.
>
> Your stakeholders aren't marketers. So how are they going to know what makes for great marketing if you don't teach them?

If Kessler is correct: if it's part of our job to teach before we execute – even if just to ensure we have the permission to execute – then we need to get better at teaching. That's a skill set in itself – one that many modern and technically skilled B2B marketers may not have in abundance.

Among other skills, teaching others at all levels across the business in order to do our jobs properly requires you to adopt these five attributes:

★ **Tune in:** To make deals with our colleagues we need to understand what we can offer that they perceive to be valuable. What are their priorities and goals? How can we help them succeed? We need to ask them; then we need to tune in.

★ **Understand the jigsaw:** It's crucial to be able to hold conversations with cross-functional colleagues like the CFO, COO and the CEO. We can't afford to glaze over or get lost when the topic of conversation drifts from marketing to, say, the balance sheet or a legal consideration. We need to understand the whole business to merit conversations with the people whose influence we need.

★ **Use the right language:** Following on from that last point, we need to be conscious of the language and terms we employ. I deal with this issue in depth elsewhere in this book, but in short, if you intend to assert a point of view, be armed with evidence and data and talk in terms of finance – it's the language of business.

★ **Be patient:** Decisions – especially those that challenge a status quo – don't happen quickly. You'll be left, often for weeks in between meetings, in a sea of ambiguity. For fear of sounding like an awful cod-motivational Facebook meme, don't drown in this sea, learn to swim in it.

★ **Know:** This is the hardest one. To teach others about marketing, we need to actually know marketing. It would help if we knew it not just from a practical, on-the-ground perspective but with some level of formal training or qualifications. Purely anecdotally, a huge number of us 'fell' into marketing and learn as we go. It might be time we committed, as an industry, to becoming professional and fully certified marketers.

22 B2Beatles: Why John, Paul, George and Ringo are perfect B2B role models

One of the themes most commonly cited by the younger marketers I interviewed for this book was a poverty of role models to look up to and learn from in B2B marketing.

Matthew Robinson, the senior director for APAC at Contentsquare, told me: 'To find inspiration I often find myself looking *outside* of B2B marketing. Maybe that says something quite worrying about us as a discipline.'

Maybe. But while we start the long process of turning B2B marketing into a better, braver and more effective business discipline, we needn't regret looking elsewhere for genius to motivate us. Our brains are not so regimented that we can only be inspired by role models who mirror the jobs we do or work in similar fields.

Creativity and inspiration aren't battery farmed. They are entirely free range. Anything that makes you feel energised or stirs your thinking is legitimate and welcome.

My B2B marketing role models are The Beatles. I'll assume you're familiar with them, though not for their B2B marketing chops. Here are a few reasons John, Paul, George and Ringo would have made for brilliant B2B marketers if they hadn't been so busy.

1. They were dogged about creating original content

The band made an early decision to write their own songs at a time when it just wasn't the done thing for recording artists.

Learning: Deciding from the outset to make originality your benchmark reaps you disproportionate benefits. It also forces you to become an ideas factory – a good habit to develop.

2. If you do steal, make it count

When The Beatles did steal other people's content, they didn't just pay tribute to what were often obscure rhythm & blues tracks. They added youth, energy, speed and urgency to turn them into iconic, Beatles standards. *Twist and Shout* wasn't a Beatles original. Nor was *Boys*, which featured Ringo's shouted 'call' vocals and John, Paul and George's 'response', sung over Ringo's manic drumming and recorded in a single, blistering take. *Dizzy Miss Lizzy* was nicked from New Orleans singer-songwriter and pianist Larry Williams. On paper, it's not that notable a song but George's searing lead guitar and John's raw, pleading vocal make it worthy.

Learning: How you transform old ideas with a fresh take will tell your market everything it needs to know about your sense of conviction, purpose and energy.

3. They *worked* to be that good

The Beatles made themselves qualified. They practised hard; we're talking Malcolm Gladwell's 'ten thousand hours' and more. In an era when the apprenticeship was a common route into work, The Beatles made five trips to Hamburg between 1960 and 1962, playing for up to eight hours a night, seven days a week. Chronicled in *The Beatles Anthology*, John Lennon said: 'We played for hours on end. Every song lasted twenty minutes and had twenty solos in it. That's what improved the playing. There was nobody to copy from' (see point 1).[23]

Learning: There's really only one way to become as good as you want them to think you are. Work hard.

---

[23] *The Beatles Anthology*. Chronicle Books, 2000.

4. They overcame obstacles

Two of the band became comfortable with their own shortcomings in ability.

George and Paul were instinctively gifted on their instruments in conventional ways others understood. John, though, had an innate rhythm all his own and was often questioned about the quality of his guitar playing. He didn't even consider himself that good. He knew his strengths and played to them. His groove and timing as a guitarist is hard to imitate.

'I'm OK,' he told a *Rolling Stone* journalist when asked about his guitar playing in 1971. 'I'm not technically good, but I can make it fucking howl and move. If you sat me with B. B. King, I'd feel silly. I'm embarrassed about my guitar playing in one way because it's very poor, but I can make a guitar speak. I can make a band drive.'[24] Similarly, Ringo's drumming was unique. Being a left-handed drummer on a right-handed kit gave his playing a rare quality because he led with his 'wrong hand'. But he also innovated 'underneath' the more vaunted work of his colleagues with drum parts all of his own. Fans commonly cite the song *Rain* as an example of his uncommon talent. Good as it is though, it's not the best example of Ringo's genius in my opinion. A listen to any one of *She Said She Said* on the *Revolver* album, *Come Together* from *Abbey Road*, *Ticket to Ride* from *Help*, *A Day in the Life* from *Sgt Pepper's Lonely Hearts Club Band* or, what, in his book *Revolution in the Head*, Ian MacDonald calls Ringo's 'indispensable foundation work' on *Strawberry Fields Forever*, would highlight why Ringo was the other Beatles' choice as drummer. Where many others aimed for a tight, crisp sound, Ringo's drumming has what drummer Abe Laboriel Jr calls a 'sloppy, swampy, falling down the stairs kind of sound – the coolest thing ever'.[25] Ringo is criticised for his drumming but drummers love him.

Learning: You possess a trait that others will define as a weakness. It's not a weakness; it's a distinction. Turn it to your advantage.

5. They knew their competitors

When you have to beat the Rolling Stones and the Beach Boys to be the best, it pushes you to insane heights. In 1966, the Stones recorded *Paint It Black*

---

[24] J. S. Wenner, *Rolling Stone*, January 1971.

[25] Rock & Roll Hall of Fame, 'World's greatest drummers salute Ringo Starr'. YouTube video, 7 July 2015. Available from www.youtube.com/watch?v=wJTjjAXDZSY [accessed 6 March 2021].

and the album *Aftermath*, which included *Under My Thumb*, *Out of Time* and *Mother's Little Helper*. The same year, the Beach Boys released *Wouldn't It Be Nice* and *Sloop John B* on the album *Pet Sounds*. The Beatles recorded *Paperback Writer* and produced the *Revolver* album. All this dazzling output was partly driven by these bands trying to outdo one another.

By contrast, in 1966 Manchester group The Hollies – inconceivably part of the same scene in the same era – produced album *For Certain Because* and singles *Bus Stop* and *Stop, Stop, Stop*; a tedious pair of bland e-book equivalents.

Learning: Find yourself a worthy competitor. Recognise and celebrate its quality internally with your team. It will spur you on.

6. They understood 'multi-channel'

The Beatles created content of the highest possible standard. Some 50 years later, young children know and sing their songs. Imagine anything you write being quoted, cited or performed five decades from now.

And they were multi-channel marketers. They recorded songs, wrote books, produced feature-length films, performed live panto on theatre stages, drew sketches and experimented with photography.

They could make any format their own – as compelling a band in a cramped, sweaty basement in Liverpool as they were in front of a 55,000-strong audience at the home of Major League Baseball team the Mets in New York City.

Learning: B2B marketing doesn't need to be restricted to the same boring channels and formats with which we're all so familiar. Here's a brief: what combination of message and media would have people citing your work, word for word, in 50 years' time?

7. They were storytellers

For four young men with a level of status and wealth that separated them from most, The Beatles – especially Paul – instinctively knew how to speak to the often humdrum lives of 'normal' people. Headlines in the *Daily Mirror* and *Daily Mail* respectively inspired the colourful poignancy of *She's Leaving Home* and *A Day in the Life*.

Elsewhere, the imagery and diverse set of characters – sometimes hilarious, other times violent or lonely – contained in the likes of *Eleanor Rigby*, *Girl*, *She Came in Through the Bathroom Window*, *Nowhere Man*, *Penny*

Lane, Norwegian Wood (This Bird Has Flown), Paperback Writer, Ob-la-di Ob-la-da, Lady Madonna, Lovely Rita, Polythene Pam, I Am the Walrus and Happiness Is a Warm Gun are now laced permanently throughout the British psyche and culture.

Learning: Use stories to create a world outside of your products and promotions. People attach to a story in ways they don't to a sales pitch.

8. The Beatles innovated wildly but their brand remained constant

The Beatles are the most 'branded' musical artist ever. Thousands of bands and artists have a widely recognised and unmistakeable sound, look and feel but The Beatles were brand masters. In their time as a group, they changed everything possible about their product and their image. From leather-clad teens, to suited and booted national treasure, to drug-experimenting mid-sixties popstars, to Yellow Submarine movie cartoon characters, to long-haired rock aristocracy and an often madcap beyond, including John and wife Yoko conducting interviews with the world's press from inside a bag, The Beatles were constantly on the move.

But you'd recognise every one of their looks. If I say 'Beatle haircut', 'Beatle boots' or 'Beatle collarless jackets', you likely have the same image in your head as I have. You can identify the band just from their silhouette on a fridge magnet.

The Beatles' brand was multi-layered and complex; it incorporated their distinct contributions and personalities: Paul's melodic bass playing, for example, or John's rebellious streak. The result was more than a branded 'product' – rather, there is a branded universe of mythology and music – broad enough for Beatles lovers of all ages and tastes to find something to feast upon.

Learning: Your brand is more than your 'look and feel'; your logo and colour palette, for example. It's far more about what you represent to your customers. As long as it holds true to the brand values or distinct positioning you offer to your community, you can experiment as much as you want with formats, colours and channel strategy.

9. They knew how to use 'branded' assets

Not only did The Beatles create their own brand, they instinctively knew how to extend their reach and accessibility through other branded assets or codes. If you haven't read or heard Professor Mark Ritson talk about brand codes, visit YouTube and type in 'Mark Ritson' and 'how Snickers turned around declining market share'.[26] The video is well worth ten minutes of your time. The Beatles 'universe' stretched to accommodate their context, their friends and, at times, their surroundings, as 'owned' 'Beatles assets': I'm thinking, for example, of Abbey Road studios and the zebra crossing outside the famous studio's front door, *The Ed Sullivan Show* in the US and the distinct shape of Paul's Hofner violin bass guitar, all of which are synonymous with The Beatles' legend.

Learning: Use context, whether unique or simply meaningful to you, as part of your brand experience. When Matthew Robinson was head of marketing at Contentsquare, his young marketing team hosted its first breakfast event. Just before the first speaker took to the stage, the venue's slide projector broke. Without it, the speakers wouldn't be able to show any of their prepared visuals. While the venue team rushed to borrow a projector from a sister hotel across London, guests – who had eaten breakfast and drunk their fill of coffee – were becoming agitated about a very delayed start to the event. Robinson needed a way to keep guests from leaving. The idea he came up with was to order in a large volume of fine champagne. It was 9am. It worked. His guests suddenly forgot why they had to be back at their respective offices, and stayed to spend more time together while drinking expensive champagne. The projector finally arrived and the event continued as planned. From then on, 'champagne breakfasts' became a regular event format for the Contentsquare UK team. It's a brand distinction. Even mistakes and emergencies can be useful brand 'stamps' that can help you become better known.

10. Their authenticity connected them more strongly to their fans

The Beatles dug deep inside themselves and their own experiences for their inspiration. The music and lyrics of *Penny Lane, Strawberry Fields Forever, Help, In My Life* and *I'm a Loser* (with its refrain of 'I'm not what I appear to be') were among their most personal and self-aware tracks.

Learning: Often, the deeper you look inside yourself and your experience to find 'real' stimulus for your content, the more it's likely to connect with your audience.

---

[26] *Marketing Week*, 'Mark Ritson on how Snickers turned around declining market share'. YouTube video, 15 July 2019. Available from www.youtube.com/watch?v=dKkXD6HicLc [accessed 6 March 2021].

11. The Beatles were brave

The Beatles were unafraid to be themselves. Though courted by the establishment, they were unconcerned by supposed social hierarchies or authority and refused to adhere to other people's 'nonsense' rules.

At various times they spoke openly (and often controversially) on their drug use, on religion and on the nonsense hype of celebrity where, if they were playing the 'PR game' right, they would have remained silent.

They refused to play to racially segregated audiences in the US in towns like Jacksonville, Florida, even though they knew their decision would confuse or anger many Americans.

Untrained in the media, they stared down or made fun of stupid questions at press conferences. Old TV footage shows that when one of them gave an answer that could be deemed controversial, none of the bandmates flinched or even, at times, looked up. They trusted and backed each other to be honest and straight-talking. When you've got that kind of support from colleagues, it breeds the strength to be you, without unnecessary PR gloss.

Learning: Your audience is sophisticated and can smell glitzy PR polish on you a mile off. PR is useful to a point but not when it gets in the way of you being real, honest and interesting.

12. They invented tirelessly, even after failing

As recording artists, The Beatles stretched the possible. They featured backwards guitar on I'm Only Sleeping and recorded a George Martin electric piano solo at half-speed before playing the tape back at double speed to create an entirely different sound on In My Life.

Importantly, they weren't deterred when their risks didn't come off. The surreal Magical Mystery Tour movie in 1967 was a critical flop but it didn't stop them stretching their imaginations again two years later, to create the Yellow Submarine film.

Learning: Exploring and taking risks appeal to our human need for advancement. If nothing else, taking a risk to try something new gets you remembered.

13. They were great at both briefing and selling in ideas

The Beatles pushed through the barriers of a four-piece rock band and, hence, needed outsiders to help them create their records. That meant harnessing the skills of strangers.

Paul said of the big orchestra crescendo on A Day in the Life:

> We told the orchestra — 'you've got fifteen bars, all you've gotta do is start on whatever is the lowest note on your instrument and by the time the end of those 15 bars has arrived, you've got to be on the top note on your instrument – we don't mind how you get there.'

'The orchestra sections have their own personalities,' explained Paul.

> The trumpets were more adventurous than anyone. They're traditionally the wags in the orchestra, the brass players, because it's thirsty work so they'd often have a little drink and stuff, whereas the strings are much more conservative as people. They all looked at each other like a little herd of sheep. 'Are you going up, when are you going up, I'm going with him, oh, he's gone...'
>
> The trumpets were all over the show. It was great.
>
> But I had to go around explaining it to everyone, 'it's a silly idea I know, but bear with us, it will work out, don't worry'...

Learning: Selling in a vision or idea is not a 'one-time' job. You have to understand your various niche audiences and then keep on talking, keep on selling. Don't stop telling everyone how it's going to work and what the result will look like. People have doubts and fears. They can be cynical. If it's your idea, you've got to be a leader.

14. They got results

The Beatles didn't just sell records by the million. They changed the world. They scared the establishment. They influenced culture. They created teenagers. They triggered mania. Their fans and stories will outlast all of them, as will their product.

Learning: Your role is to do great marketing. Your job is to help grow the company and sell product. Your 'results'? What you'll be known and remembered for by 'the end'? Well, that's up to you.

23 Persuasion and profitability

Pitching anything out of the ordinary for consideration as the next marketing activity to a room of sales, operations and engineering colleagues is an experience that still, after years of doing it, leaves me tasting the nerves in my mouth in the moments before my presentation.

There's a look in their eyes I dread seeing as I'm in full persuasive mode. It's a look that blends confusion and disdain. They don't care (and nor should they) that their CEO may have excitedly signed off on the idea they're watching me rant at them. It barely matters to them that I'm showing them that something similar I've done before has been successful.

They just don't get it. Especially if what I'm sharing *seemingly* has little to do with the company or the product – perhaps it's more about the customer, the challenges the customer faces or the aspirations they have; maybe the idea aims to pull a community together around a universal industry issue. There's a flawed assumption made by many people in business that being brave creatively, telling stories about things other than your product or just having a bit more fun detracts from the important job of focusing on revenue and profit.

The confused part of my audience's response I can handle. Sometimes it's a useful sign I need to be more clear. But after years of sales or technical people staring blankly back at me, I've learned initial success in these situations is often winning over a third of the room, with another third staunchly ambivalent until they see the campaign or activity roll out, make us famous and, in turn, add grease to their sales efforts. The remaining third of my colleagues often leave the room unconvinced and hoping never to find themselves alone in an elevator with me. Yep, I can handle the confusion part.

When you have to tell them marketing is more hard-nosed and commercial than sales...

What continues to intrigue me is the disdain. Their sentiment seems to be: 'We're trying to run a business here – why are we allocating resource to these guys in marketing that just want to have fun?'

People whose roles rely on them thinking in a logical and linear way sometimes struggle to see that making B2B marketing more interesting, fun or creative is a commercial endeavour – a cold, hard, pragmatic calculation.

Building a strong, desirable brand or even just committing to sustained exposure to make your company's name and promotions memorable generates more powerful long-term growth than any sales team.

Even the strongest sales function spends time focusing on individual deals and chasing leads one by one. If marketing does its job right, chasing individual leads becomes less critical a task. A strong, relevant brand investing in share of voice with a relevant, persuasive proposition attracts inbound enquiries in volumes, from already-warm prospects.

Still, the disdain and sometimes distrust is a response even the most successful B2B marketers are used to. Doug Kessler's profile in B2B couldn't be much higher. The New Yorker began his career at ad agency Ogilvy before switching to B2B. His firm Velocity Partners helps some of the bravest and most successful B2B companies out there with positioning, digital and content marketing.

Kessler states that throughout his career there's always been a 'hard-nosed sales guy' sitting somewhere near him who views him as a 'snowflake':

> It's ironic that this guy sees me as the creative snowflake. I'm way more hard-nosed than he is. His activities are all geared towards short term goals, and, if we're honest, have a questionable hit-rate. And yet he's pointing at me, complaining there's not enough space in my marketing given over to selling the product.

> All the while, I know what works and what I do works. And right now, shoving your product in people's faces is not what works. And the longer and more you invest in proper marketing, once you've put this stuff in place, the better it performs. So I hate feeling pitted against those damn sales guys. They're not educated about what actually works and what creates the better lead.

> If we could help them along that curve, we'd align better because we'd all understand what each part of the marketing mix is supposed to be doing.

Growth while you sleep

I know two brothers who have built a brilliant global business. Before Richard and Jonny Townsend created Circus Street, which delivers interactive digital training courses to teams in enterprise companies around the world, they were looking for an idea for a business that would make money 'while they sleep'.

Brand awareness is the growth activity that works while you sleep. Twinned with (rather than as a replacement for) sales activation, it makes for a devastating combination.

Binet and Field's earlier cited research of 2019 defines sales activation as any that gets you 'an immediate response', usually tightly targeted on 'hot prospects' and typified by performance marketing, incentives and most of your digital activity.

'ROIs can be high', the report states, 'but it is unlikely to be very memorable, so effects don't last long and do little to foster long-term growth'.

'By contrast,' say Binet and Field, 'top of the funnel activity excels at driving long-term growth', employing emotion to create 'long-term memories and associations that continue to influence purchase decisions long after the advertising runs'.[27]

We've failed at proving marketing profitability – so far…

Why, as B2B marketers and organisations, have we so failed to appreciate or realise the devastating potential of twinning both long- and short-term marketing activity?

Perhaps the bigger question is: what do we do with the information now that we have it? How are we going to do things differently and put it into action?

'We're not', predicts Professor Mark Ritson, *Marketing Week* columnist and the man behind the *Marketing Week* mini-MBA which trains and qualifies thousands of marketers globally every year.

Ritson, an admirer of Binet and Field's work, states:

---

[27] The B2B Institute, *5 Principles of Growth in B2B Marketing: Empirical Observations on B2B Effectiveness*. LinkedIn, 2019. Available from https://business.linkedin.com/marketing-solutions/b2b-institute/marketing-as-growth [accessed 6 March 2021].

Marketing's got a pretty small echo chamber which, if you're not careful, you start to believe is the whole of marketing. The reality is most B2B marketers have never heard of Field or Binet, have no idea what any of this means and wouldn't know how to apply it if they did.

The culture of sales and the short-termism is so strong in B2B, it would take a lot to dislodge it.

So I don't think it will have a massive impact, in and of itself, even though it was great work.

I press Ritson – ever the realist – for a sunnier takeaway and he agrees that a clearer understanding of where marketing and sales activities should play along the sales funnel would be his 'no-brainer' start towards greater commercial success.

'Occupy the part of the funnel where you're most effective'

Mark Ritson continues:

It's eluded most people in B2B that the sales team shouldn't be anywhere near the top of the funnel but you don't really want marketing doing sales activation at the bottom of the funnel either.

B2B outfits generally have a very decent sales team and a strong product, so marketers should move out of the way at the bottom of the funnel and let a good sales force do the business for you. Nothing beats a really good, well-run sales team at activation, account management, relationships and closing the deal.

Meanwhile, I think it's bananas to not focus on the top of funnel from a marketing point of view – that's where you can get some real growth for your company and where you'll be respected for your commercial contribution.

Whatever we identify as individual marketers that will change our businesses for the better and braver, we face a struggle in articulating it to the rest of our organisations. Conversations must be based on profitability and market share and almost nothing else.

Ultimately, until we can actually demonstrate proof (there are few more frustrating truths than the Steve Jobs quote about only being able to 'fully connect the dots backwards'), the way we're going to drive change is to frame the things we want to do in terms of financial gain. As Ritson comments:

Trying to get B2B companies to even address the fact that the best way to spend the money is on long-term stuff will take at least two years.

Spending almost half the marketing budget on top of the funnel brand awareness is currently unimaginable to most of them. The message that still doesn't get through enough is that the reason you should do it is it would make you loads more money.

A case study in cost effectiveness

Investing properly in brand doesn't just make you new money, it helps you save on costs too. The more distinct and recognisable you are to your market through your unmistakeable and unique tone of voice (see next chapter), the less money you have to spend cutting through the noise.

As former global brand director for B2B insurance firm Hiscox, Annabel Venner worked with businesses throughout Europe, the US and Asia. As she notes:

We started investing in our brands in Asia and sure enough, more people arrived at our websites after searching on the 'brand term'. The cost of building on a brand term is a tenth of bidding on a generic industry term. Investing in brands is so much more cost effective and that's a great example. Bidding against everybody else for generic terms on Google is dumb. The only winner there is Google. It's so great to share stories like that where we've done something that worked so well. It becomes a powerful case study to show around the business to get other people thinking on our terms.

***

I only really learned this as I got older and more experienced but becoming good at the art of persuasion makes up about half the job in B2B marketing if not more. Especially when you're new in a job and configuring your team and function to fit the approach that makes most sense to you.

There's a need to pitch (and continuously evolve) the same marketing strategy or campaign idea several times – often using different tailored content for a meeting, depending on who you're sitting in a room trying to convince.

I reflect often that I'm grateful for the listening, pitching, investigative and storytelling skills I honed as a newspaper and magazine journalist in a former career.

There are many skills I don't have but I do know this: if you want to be an effective B2B marketing leader; one who's respected and valued across the business, you need to learn to become 'the great persuader'.

24 Stop being a marketer: Start being a go-to-marketer

At one point, my Rebeltech co-founder Nicole Lyons and I stopped calling ourselves a B2B tech marketing agency and started referring to ourselves and our offer as a go-to-market agency.

We didn't just become instantly more popular; we started hearing from a different kind of customer with more interesting briefs.

Go-to-market (GTM) strategy clearly can't be 'owned' by marketing. But marketing should absolutely play a significant role in the GTM plan and can grow its role and involvement in the business by offering more of a contribution to that conversation.

When tech market intelligence platform CB Insights published a list of 'The top 20 reasons startups fail', half of them were go-to-market failures, including 'no market need for product', 'pricing/cost issues', 'ignoring customers' and 'poor marketing'.[28]

Making marketing more central to the go-to-market discussion gives us an opportunity to collaborate with the sales, product marketing, customer success and product teams on an equal footing.

---

[28] CB Insights, 'The top 20 reasons startups fail', 6 November 2019. Available from www.cbinsights.com/research/startup-failure-reasons-top/ [accessed 6 March 2021].

'Marketing owns the customer... right? What's that? Oh'

One of the conversations I had with many of the contributors to this book was that the justification marketing has always put forward for influence within the business is that marketing 'owns' the customer.

The problem is, we really don't. Not in B2B.

Certainly in B2B tech organisations, it's typical for the marketing function to feel like the department kept furthest away from the customer. Sales obviously owns a relationship with customers, along with the client and customer success teams. Even the product team gets regular exposure to customers to discuss the roadmap and help solve tech issues.

Besides the odd grabbed opportunity for conversations with your customers when they come to speak at your own company's events or dinners, it's very easy to get through an entire year as a B2B tech marketer without meeting any of your customers.

The consensus among all of the contributors to this book was that this must change; that customer input to our work is essential.

How to get closer to your customers, starting now

Margaret Molloy of Siegel+Gale agrees that it's essential for B2B marketers to have independent relationships with customers. 'You'll learn so much more that's useful to you from a direct customer conversation than you will from hearing customer feedback second-hand,' she says. 'But there's another reason: you being seen by your colleagues bringing customers and users into the building is incredibly powerful. First-hand customer accounts is the fastest way to unlock an argument over internal strategy.'

Molloy lists a number of tactics she's seen used to bring marketers closer to customers:

1. Insist on getting access to customers. And if you're blocked by someone? Well, drop them a line anyway.

2. Simply ask to take a customer out for a coffee. Or create a 'lunch with the customer' programme where you meet a different customer every Friday.

3. Tell a customer you need to tap their experience for some research or interview them for your next piece of marketing collateral.

4. Set up a customer advisory panel. Your customers will be flattered and your business will love you for it.

5. Build a campaign around your product's power users or maybe the users that want to use a certain subset of the features.

Email, when done right, can also be a perfectly good channel through which to properly engage customers, says Ann Handley, chief content officer at MarketingProfs.

Handley uses her bi-weekly newsletter to have a genuine relationship with her followers. Using email comes easily to Handley. Her advice: 'You want a better newsletter? Focus on the letter, not just on the news.' She continues:

> The email newsletter is vastly undervalued in B2B organisations. Using the email newsletter as a tool to not just distribute your content and focus on the news part of it, but also on the letter part – that's a mistake lots of marketers make in the B2B space.
>
> They don't leverage the email newsletter tool to hear back from customers and prospects; instead, it's just about distributing their own content. The 'two-way communication' opportunity of a newsletter is something that's very useful to nurture customers and to your future marketing programmes.

I've heard it said that the engineering teams have the level of influence they do in B2B tech businesses because 'code wins arguments'.

Code doesn't win arguments. Customers do.

We have to assert ourselves. If I had to pick one single piece of advice from everything in this book, one tweak a B2B marketer should make to their week-to-week existence that would generate the biggest impact on their level of internal influence, it would be to find a way of having regular one-to-one conversations with customers.

25 Frankenstein's monsters in Salt Lake City: A story

11am, 10 March 2015

I'm standing in the bright morning sunshine outside the Salt Palace Convention Center in Salt Lake City watching 20 Frankenstein's monsters doing the dance to Michael Jackson's *Thriller*.

It's days like this that are why I sometimes struggle to explain to friends and family exactly what I do for a living. For these are my Frankenstein's monsters. They came to my Salt Lake City Airbnb 'safe house' to be briefed this morning at 5am; 25 actors all answered a local newspaper ad for '*large male actors; two-day job; details shared on arrival*'.

Coffee and pastries were served while professional make-up artists painstakingly turned them into monsters. My two colleagues and I talked excitedly at them as they underwent their transformation.

Our mission for the next two days is a 'benign and friendly' hijack of the annual Adobe Summit, an event which will host thousands of delegates, all potential customers of ours. I work for Qubit, the leading enterprise personalisation and customer experience software.

Two weeks earlier

Qubit HQ, London

I answer the phone at my desk. It's internal, the CEO's assistant. She asks me to come to his office immediately. I assume I'm in trouble. On the way up to the next floor, I try to recall any screw-up that might just now have been discovered. Nothing comes to mind.

When I enter the CEO's office, he is there with three others sitting around the table. They all stop talking when I enter. 'Close the door please, Mark.'

I sit. 'Mark, we need you to go to Utah, but before you do we need you first to go to New York for a few days. You might have to be away for about 10 days – is that going to be ok with your family? We need you to do something for us.'

Intrigued and feeling a bit like 007, I said I could make it work.

'Great stuff, Mark. Now, what we're about to tell you can't be shared with anyone else in the company besides the people in this room and the team you pick in New York. Everyone else has to stay in the dark.'

I'll be honest. If you want to get me excited about and bought into a project, that's the way to start the brief.

Here's what they told me:

'Every year Adobe holds a huge digital summit in the US. In exactly a fortnight, around 5,000 delegates are due to arrive in Salt Lake City for two days. Those delegates are our potential customers. We want you to somehow make a big noise and we think we've got an idea as to how you can do it.'

'By the way,' the CEO added, 'not everybody in this room thinks this is a good plan.'

The plan

Adobe is a giant. At the time, it didn't even know Qubit existed, let alone recognise in us a competitor. Without breaking any laws or annoying any of the delegates or ruining their experience (they were there, after all, to drink the Adobe Kool-Aid and had paid handsomely to do so), we wanted to draw the delegates' attention to one specific differentiator between our products.

Qubit's cloud-based customer experience and personalisation suite was built as an integrated offer from the ground up and around the customer's needs.

Adobe's customer cloud was the result of a series of acquisitions of products that were never designed or built to work together, all formed into what we planned to call a 'Frankencloud'.

A bit naughty but not untrue.

We were going to put a load of Frankenstein's monsters outside the Adobe show, greeting customers as they got off their coaches and out of their taxi cabs.

We would be entertaining, as opposed to in any way threatening, and somehow we would compel them to type DumpFrank.com into their cell phone internet browsers before they got to the door of the summit to enter Adobe's world.

Now, nothing exists at the web destination of DumpFrank.com. Then, within days of hatching this plan at the end of February 2015, we'd created a fast, easy, 'four swipe' microsite. It led a user through a series of amusing visuals, offering reasons why a Frankencloud might not be a good choice of romantic (or business) partner and why if you wanted to 'Dump Frank' there are other options out there that could make you happy. The last swipe brought users to a form with which they could book a Qubit demo.

Within days, I was in our New York HQ, working quietly with two brilliant marketing colleagues, Charlton Lamb and Andrew Zahornacky. Some of the discussions that took place:

★ We need a local base for the two days that the summit is taking place. Every hotel room in Salt Lake City is booked but in any case we need something larger; big enough for about 20 people and a make-up crew.

★ We need transport and two days' worth of food for the actors…

★ Erm, and we also need the actors… is there an acting or theatre school nearby?

★ How do we find a professional 'movie-level' make-up crew and what can we tell them without letting too much out of the bag?

★ What do we need to make ourselves legally safe so we don't just get moved on by the police? We need some sort of permit from the local council that allows us to bring 20 Frankenstein's monsters onto the public sidewalks. (Yes, reader, it turns out those permits actually exist.)

★ Is everything set up digitally? The microsite? The social feeds?

★ We have to talk about the risks here. This could massively backfire. We risk looking 'small' and also pretty stupid. Guerrilla marketing stunts fill me with dread. I worry that what we are attempting may simply not work or, worse, end up harming our brand. What are we going to do to mitigate that risk? Have any of us had experience managing 20 Frankenstein's monsters in a public space? What…? None of us?

8am, 10 March, 2015: The Airbnb, Salt Lake City, Utah

We're about to leave our 'safe house'. The Frankenstein's monsters all look incredible and the actors underneath the make-up are all game.

Outside the house, the first nervous argument breaks out. We have too many Frankenstein's monsters to squeeze into our van and yet it takes us way too long to agree that we're going to have to do two journeys to the conference centre. But then nobody slept well last night and we've been up since 4am so fatigue and nerves are mixing with adrenaline and coffee to generate a growing buzz. Our van has blacked-out windows which, for some reason, I find exciting. I'm in the passenger seat at the front. The engine is on; I turn around to watch as the gruesome, green monsters in the back sensibly belt themselves in.

10.30am: Outside the Adobe Summit

This is hilarious. Our 20 monsters are collecting nothing but goodwill and love in the form of hundreds of hugs, high-fives and selfies from marketers heading into the summit.

We've asked them not to speak to delegates but instead to amuse, in any 'non-threatening' way possible. New ideas to do so have required us to run around the city collecting 'props'.

They've handed out roses. They've hula hooped. They've hand-signalled coach drivers into parking spots and they've hijacked snacks-carts and food vans to serve breakfast to hungry delegates.

Each of them is wearing our DumpFrank.com t-shirts and our microsite is getting a ton of traffic.

Adobe people have come outside to move us on and ended up taking selfies with us for their kids. Police officers have come to question us and walked away with selfies of their own.

We have a film crew on-site with a drone camera to capture everything. Within 24 hours they deliver us a 60-second film which we target at our audience on YouTube. Within a couple of weeks, they will also send a two-minute 'the making of' video.

Two days of haring around trying to charm Adobe delegates later, we pack up and leave town. Apart from the constant, face-to-face engagement we'd enjoyed with our target audience and a load of organic social media activity, we really had no idea how well we'd done.

Mark Choueke
@MarkChoueke

Marketers attending the #adobesummit are showing some Frankenstein love. Visit DumpFrank.com to see why.

Results

The results we know about include an estimated ROI (in both direct and indirect new business that we could attribute to the stunt) of about 30:1.

The long tail of brand awareness and positive sentiment was also significant.

★ The two YouTube videos garnered more than 75,000 views in the week of the activity and the month after.

★ Clients and prospects told us delegates inside the summit were only talking about one thing in their coffee breaks: 'those crazy Frankensteins outside'.

★ One client told us vendors try to make noise at the Adobe Summit every year but this stunt got noticed like no other. We sent DumpFrank t-shirts and masks out to clients and prospects on request.

★ We hired senior sales executives from Adobe following the stunt. They told us that after DumpFrank, Adobe had developed 'How to beat Qubit in a pitch' training sessions for their sales teams.

I tell this story not just because it's the most fun I've ever had doing B2B marketing. The idea was incredibly brave and, indeed, acknowledged as a business risk while it was still only that – 'someone's idea'. But the management of a brilliant and credible company felt it was worth doing in order to raise our profile among a supremely targeted audience. The success of the stunt, it was felt, would hinge on the tone of the activity on the ground – can we entertain delegates without annoying them? Is the message clear enough to get us good volumes of clicks onto our microsite?

We managed the entire activity carefully and were committed throughout to shutting the whole thing down immediately if anything looked like it was about to go downhill or cause trouble.

As it happened, the bravery and risk paid off. The DumpFrank activity turned out to be what our customers wanted to talk to us about that year. It galvanised our people across all our markets and gave us the confidence to explore new and braver ways of telling our stories to the market in subsequent years. Quantifying the value of that isn't easy but when you try something this big – this brave – and it works?

You never look back.

26 Bravery as a strategy:
A happiness mindset

The person you are in the first weeks of a new job is the most powerful B2B marketer you'll ever be. The learning curve in a new role is steep and multi-faceted but incredibly energising.

Your new colleagues are keen to get in touch and welcome you personally, interested to get their first measure of what you might bring to the fold. You're high with confidence for the validation you were just given in being hired, and the excitement and positivity you feel is so tangible it's virtually prickling your skin.

The result of all this is that you do something very few of us continue doing beyond that honeymoon period.

You ask questions.

You've got not just the confidence but the licence as a newbie to ask as many 'dumb questions' as you want. Subsequently, every meeting sees you tuned in and ravenous for new information to process and analyse. You ask questions of everybody.

And it feels great. Not just to you but to your organisation. Your colleagues are refreshed to get the chance to confirm, review and substantiate their individual roles, the wider mechanics of the business and how things work; they tell you which things are going right but, importantly, which tend not to go so well. When you ask why a particular thing is broken, they shrug and tell you nobody is taking responsibility to fix the problem.

When that happens, it's an invitation. They're saying: 'We all know this thing isn't working, but none of us feel we have the energy or permission to sort it. Maybe that person could be you?'

When you're meeting huge numbers of new colleagues for the first time over the first three months or so, you're going to hear this scenario hundreds of times over. Sometimes it may be a marketing thing, other times it will be a product or sales problem. Often it will be a relationships and communications glitch.

Whatever the nature of the problems you learn about, you become a walking logbook of headaches across your company. It's a list you could spend the next year raising with the right people and helping to solve. Think what a hero you'd be. Consider what it would mean for you if everyone across the organisation saw you less specifically as the new marketer and more simply: 'someone to look up to'; 'someone I could ask for help'; 'someone with influence who knows how to remove obstacles and solve problems'.

In time, however, as you start to become part of the furniture (is that anyone else's perception, do you think? Or just yours?), that power inevitably leaves you. You stop asking tough questions; you cease pointing out what's secretly obvious to everyone in the name of making positive change. You become just 'another great colleague'.

Siegel+Gale CMO Margaret Molloy talks about this: 'People assume in this world of urgency they have to get up to speed fast. Sometimes the implication of that is you stop asking questions because you're supposed to be a "quick study". Unfortunately, by denying yourself the opportunity to stay "new", you're shutting off your bravery.'

Should bravery be taught on marketing courses?

My children go to a great school in north London. It's a new school – it filled all of its year groups for the first time last year.

When my wife and I were looking for the right school, we had the same stark moment of realisation that I reckon occurs to all parents doing the same thing.

'How do you recognise the right learning and preparation for your kids' future when you don't have a clue what that future is going to look like?'

Forecasters commonly suggest half the jobs our children will make a living from have not yet been invented.

How, then, do we best prepare our kids to thrive in a working world that will almost certainly bear little resemblance to the one we operate in and understand?

The school we eventually got our kids into had a strong answer. While obviously committed to academic achievement, the school is keen to develop '21st century learning skills' for an age where information is a mere Google search away.

These skills include creativity, innovation, critical thinking and problem solving, communication and collaboration, familiarity with technology, good citizenship, volunteerism, mutual responsibility and an ability to build positive relationships.

The list also included teaching the children how and when to take calculated risks.

Schools are teaching our kids the value of taking risks.

I think that's brilliant. It made me think about whether 'bravery' should be on the curriculum of marketing courses, alongside brand management theory, digital marketing skills and media planning and buying.

Such an inclusion on the curriculum for new marketers would be saying: 'We can't tell you about the environment you'll have to navigate, but we're determined to give you the best chance of navigating it.'

'Risk-free' marketing: The most expensive marketing money can buy

It's largely an absence of bravery or risk that means so much of B2B marketing isn't worth the money paid for it.

By focusing so heavily on channels and tactics rather than story, mission or a strong, emotive stance on an issue, our marketing is forgettable for the recipient and often joyless for us to create.

Our bosses wonder why we create marketing that is virtually invisible.

And our brands – the very thing a marketer is there to protect and promote – are expressed in bland, colourless terms.

We're literally inviting our customers to disregard us.

Ironically, marketers and CEOs that end up in this unhappy situation often believe they are being frugal when briefing their agency or designing their marketing strategies.

Maybe they begin those processes with bold marketing outcomes in mind but, gradually, the closer these marketers get to signing off on a new campaign, the more they lose sight of what they need their marketing and PR to achieve.

Their perspective shrinks; they end up building marketing strategies around cost rather than outcomes, cutting investment to a point where their marketing programme feels relatively risk-free.

Unfortunately, that's often the point at which a marketing plan won't achieve anything even vaguely useful.

Worse, for an agency or marketer hell-bent on delivering impact, the CEO is often so bored after all the 'incremental marketing shrink' that he or she has stopped caring about marketing altogether.

Bravery as a strategy

What happens then? Campaign catch-up meetings start getting postponed or missed; marketing activity becomes reprioritised as demands from struggling sales teams get louder; updates with marketing teams or agencies become fixated upon stagnant spreadsheets and 'WIP' lists, despised by everyone.

The goal is no longer business transformation as it was before; it's now merely the watered-down case study or the chase for some PR coverage of 'that blog'.

A lack of ambition in marketing means trouble. If your marketing plan is little other than the current e-book series, a thought leadership white paper and some webinars; if you don't talk in a breathlessly excited tone about the story or rallying call behind that content and how it's uniquely your brand that can pull it off – well, you don't have much. You've got some stuff that nobody, including yourself, gives two hoots about.

So for a couple of years now, starting with the clients we worked with at Rebeltech, I've been talking about 'Bravery as a strategy'. Bravery delivers visibility and volume. It's a force multiplier for marketing. There's no scientific formula with which you can forecast the effects of being braver with your marketing – cited elsewhere in this book, there's only the Steve Jobs 'connecting the dots looking backwards' quote to offer as encouragement until you've experienced the disproportionate effects for yourself.

Here's my 'Bravery as a strategy' checklist as it currently stands for anyone wanting to join me in exploring if we can take B2B marketing from Boring2Brave.

1 Make bravery your superpower: Bravery appeals to people. We're drawn to those who demonstrate courage. We can't help it. We love their stories and want to be inspired by them. In contrast, fear is pungent. Your customers can smell it. Them clocking your organisation for being bloodless and lacking distinction or heart is the last time they'll think about you.

2   Commit: Scaling up your marketing ambition is impossible if you don't care. Invest your commitment, creativity and craft to your marketing and you'll find your budget restrictions matter less.

3   Break rules: Rules are only important to the person or organisation that made them up. According to Sam Conniff, author of *Be More Pirate*,[29] becoming a 'professional rule breaker' is now the number-one skill we need to master for success. Or put it another way: do you want to be Han Solo or C-3PO? Rules that are clever, inclusive and encourage behaviours you believe in? No problem. Rules though that are dumb, corrupt or installed out of fear? They make fools of us all. Within reason and where you can get away with it, break them.

4   Talk normal: Startups and scale-ups, stop writing in tech-speak. At best, you come across as vague when your prospects and customers want only clarity. At worst, you sound stuffy and pretentious. You're supposed to be the disruptor. You're the alternative to the guys in pinstripes. Start sounding like it.

5   Think far ahead: Look at the whole journey of the content, PR or sales collateral you're creating. It's worth nothing if it never makes its way into the hands of your prospects. And once they've got hold of your brilliant content? What then? How are you going to surprise them next?

6   Say something: And while we're on the subject of content, forget about a content calendar until you've figured out the story behind it. What's the message you want remembered by listeners to your podcast, viewers of your slideshare or attendees of your event? Story beats content – every time.

7   Inject creativity: Not all B2B marketing plans need look the same. Homogeneity is crushing and counter-productive. Creativity brings unreasonable advantage to those bold enough to wield it. Creativity is the experimental, exciting stuff you allow yourself to consider after a decision to be brave. It comes from the ambition to do something different and outstanding; to do or say something others wouldn't.

8   Stand up: This is the most important tip. You ready? Believe in marketing. Stand up to sales and product. Stop allowing them to be your editors. Support them but don't *serve* them. You know marketing better than they do. You get narrative, story, content, media, engagement and you understand the customer. Or if you don't, then make it your business to.

---

[29] S. Conniff, *Be More Pirate*. Penguin Books, 2018.

26½   Conclusion

When you write a book of about 50,000 words, you end up writing more like double that number and having to cull. A lot of detail is lost along with a few ideas and then a ton of rambling, 'late-night' content that the world should be grateful never saw the light of day.

Other things were culled too though. Elements that would have perhaps made this more of a conventional business book with step-by-step specifics and particulars for every section on exactly how to enact what I'm advocating we strive for.

This book is never going to be – could never be – the definitive guidebook for changing the trajectory and fortunes of your B2B marketing; there's a lot of discussion and explainers missing for it to be that.

What it is intended to be is a starter-gun on us all changing B2B marketing together. As I said when I pitched it to my publisher Alison Jones at Practical Inspiration, 'part manifesto, part how-to and part case study'.

This won't be the only trigger for better and braver B2B marketing starting when you get back to your desk at 9am tomorrow; nor is it the only attempted rallying-cry available on the shelves of your nearest bookstore.

What I hope it will be is some initial inspiration for anyone that has felt or does feel at work like I have in various jobs. Sometimes we're nothing more than 'an interesting misfit', an 'often-loved-but-not-always-understood' ideas machine.

Other times we can, I guess, be quite annoying for colleagues. One person's definition of 'restlessly but constructively discontent' can be seen by another as 'oh my God, does this guy ever stop asking bloody questions?'

But occasionally, and I've been lucky to have more than my fair share of these, you find the job, the company or even just the boss who knows your value and is determined to hold on to you at all costs. Someone who knows there is absolutely nobody else on the team with your perspective, skill-set and ability to create 'something out of nothing' or change things up for the better.

I know there are plenty of you out there because I've met a good many of you. You might not always fit comfortably into how organisations feel they have to work but you can find the right blend of compliance and defiance.

'Compliance' because most good changes are built on compromise, incremental steps and bringing people with you (but also 'compliance' because you need to keep your job, right?). And 'defiance' because without people like you, companies and business practices never get better.

Giving B2B marketing the chance to be more creative, more memorable, more effective and more fun is the responsibility of many. No single blog, podcast, conference speech or book was ever going to be the thing that convinces a global industry that there's more for the taking with a bit of hard work.

Rather, genuine change will come when two things occur:

1   When there are enough of us having a series of conversations so that we don't all feel like 'lone, wide-eyed crazies'.

2   When we've developed and gathered enough proof and evidence between us to build a sturdy and undeniable business case to take B2B marketing from a drab and frustrating 'boring' to a dynamic and hugely profitable 'brave'.

Best of luck. Keep in touch.

Mark

Boring2Brave.com

About the author

Mark is the marketing director at leading referral marketing platform Mention Me. A former award-winning journalist, Mark has since built a reputation as a leader at the heart of the global B2B marketing and communications arena. He's been the 'media', the 'agency' and the 'brand'; has operated within large corporates and startups alike and co-founded successful B2B tech marketing agency Rebeltech. Either as a consultant or in-house, Mark has served more than 50 B2B technology companies globally, spanning retail, ecommerce, martech, adtech, fintech, regtech, logistics and travel. In his previous career, Mark was editor of *Marketing Week* magazine and, earlier, B2B-focused marketing titles *Precision Marketing* and *Data Strategy* and was a business correspondent on newspaper *The Sunday Telegraph*. He'd give it all up tomorrow if there was even half a chance of him playing for Liverpool FC. He just recently started to accept that this probably isn't going to happen. (Though he still believes he could do a job.)

Acknowledgements

This book owes its existence to many people.

I'll start with the main one. This book is for dad and mum. Talk about brave.

Thank you, mum, for all your support, guidance and love. I'm so sorry dad didn't make it to see Boring2Brave published. I'm quite sure he would have seen his influence all over it, and just as sure he wouldn't have accepted an ounce of the credit that would have been rightfully his.

The opportunity to write Boring2Brave occurred during the first UK national Covid-19 lockdown in 2020. 'What a stroke of luck…' you might think. 'All that spare time at home to write…' It was nothing of the sort. Three lockdowns in the subsequent months may have promised us all so much extra 'time': time at home to spend with our families, 'new' time that we would have spent commuting and so on.

Well, some of that stuff happened but, honestly, if you were there, you'll also know the lockdown environment was consistently chaotic. My kids were aged seven and four. My beloved sister Jo came to live with us. I was working up to 12 hours a day for clients on Zoom calls and my wife and sister also worked full-time. Together we were trying to 'home-school' as well as keep the house functioning and clean.

So sincerest apologies and loving, grateful thanks must go to my family for all those hours I spent hidden away in our home office/laundry room, trying to get these words together.

In particular, to Deborah, who could run our household without me but still seems to want me around, I love you. Thank you for supporting me through this brilliant (and partly ego-driven) affair.

Solomon and Matilda. You drive me mad but also make me laugh hard every single day. My greatest achievement and honour is being your dad. You're both beautiful, ridiculous, hilarious and way smarter than I'll ever be. If you got this far in the book (which I doubt), I love the pair of you madly.

A heartfelt thank you also to James Clifford, Gary Benardout and Joby Blume, three dear friends who believed in me enough to back Rebeltech and have supported me since with their time, wisdom and kindness.

To Ian Abrams, who unfailingly backed and looked out for me throughout my career and to Elise Ludwin too – neither Ian nor Elise hesitated for a moment in coming forward to invest in Rebeltech. Thank you.

To Nic, my business partner (in name only for now) – thanks for setting me on this course. Let me know when you have the 'next idea' and I'll be there.

To a brilliant PR named Lucy Werner. You got me started. You advertised Alison Jones's wonderful book proposal course and then took my call that weekend to encourage me over the line.

To Wendy Webb, my favourite design partner from way back on our days together at Marketing Week, who created the excellent Boring2Brave logo and branding.

To Andrew Logan, who founded and runs the magnificent digital marketing business Floww. Andrew watched me struggle for weeks with the Boring2Brave.com website, before taking it off me and then giving it back half an hour later in its current form.

And finally, to the simply incredible Alison Jones and the team at Practical Inspiration Publishing. Alison, you're an absolute powerhouse of support, guidance and encouragement. Thanks also to Shell Cooper, Michelle Charman, Judith Wise and all the editors, designers and partners who are lucky enough to work with you. God only knows what my lockdowns would have been like without you all.

And to every single one of you brilliant marketing leaders and experts who contributed to this book. I used as much of the gold you gave me as I could, but sadly sometimes there just wasn't the room or the editorial reason to include something you said that blew me away. Over our many lockdown Zoom calls, you made me think, laugh and write. I hope you all get something out of one another's words in the pages of Boring2Brave.